THE TWILIGHT OF
PLUTO

"John Michael Greer is clearly a top-notch astrologer, scholar, and, like Richard Tarnas, a historian with a love of cosmic beauty. *The Twilight of Pluto* is not only the history of astrology but also the astrology of history. Greer brilliantly demonstrates the mirror of planet and culture, as Pluto moves from theory to discovery to planetary acceptance and then fall and demotion . . . paradigm-shifting insights! I especially appreciate his bold and positive predictions as the Plutonian era fades. Absolutely fascinating! Once I began reading I couldn't stop."

FREDERICK HAMILTON BAKER, ASTROLOGER AND AUTHOR OF
ALCHEMICAL TANTRIC ASTROLOGY

"In this relatively small volume, John Michael Greer accomplishes major feats, both intellectual and spiritual. Firstly, he has the scholarly wisdom to place planetary discoveries within the widest possible context, reminding us that the discovery of the visible planets is really the 'Big Bang' of Civilization. Then he masterfully applies the alchemical formula *solve et coagula* to break apart the more modern discoveries, purifying and distilling our understanding of them, before putting them back together into a hopeful new form, using the esoteric tools and cunning for which he's well known. The result is medicine, in the truest sense of the word."

GARY P. CATON, ASTROLOGER, AUTHOR OF
HERMETICA TRIPTYCHA, AND HOST OF
THE *HERMETIC ASTROLOGY PODCAST*

THE TWILIGHT OF
PLUTO

ASTROLOGY AND
THE RISE AND FALL OF
PLANETARY INFLUENCES

JOHN MICHAEL GREER

Inner Traditions
Rochester, Vermont

Inner Traditions
One Park Street
Rochester, Vermont 05767
www.InnerTraditions.com

Text stock is SFI certified

Cataloging-in-Publication Data for this title is available from the Library of Congress

ISBN 978-1-64411-311-0 (print)
ISBN 978-1-64411-312-7 (ebook)

Printed and bound in the United States by Lake Book Manufacturing, Inc.
The text stock is SFI certified. The Sustainable Forestry Initiative® program
promotes sustainable forest management.

10 9 8 7 6 5 4 3 2 1

Text design and layout by Debbie Glogover
This book was typeset in Garamond Premier Pro with Gill Sans MT Pro,
Nocturne Serif and Posterama Text used as display typefaces

To send correspondence to the author of this book, mail a first-class letter to the
author c/o Inner Traditions • Bear & Company, One Park Street, Rochester, VT
05767, and we will forward the communication, or contact the author directly at
www.ecosophia.net.

Contents

Introduction

On August 26, 2006, members of the International Astronomical Union filed into a hall in Prague for the last session of the organization's triennial meeting. Normally there's nothing duller in the world of astronomy. After two weeks of papers, panels, informal discussions, and social events, the final afternoon session of the IAU meeting typically attracts only a handful of attendees, most of them elected officers of the organization, who take care of necessary business—voting in new members, passing resolutions, rubberstamping decisions already made by consensus within the field—and then head for the hotel bar or the next flight home.

That day was different. There were still nine hundred new members to be voted in, and four uncontroversial resolutions to pass, covering such edge-of-the-seat issues as how to define the ecliptic and whether or not the IAU would officially endorse the Washington Charter for Communicating Astronomy with the Public. The last two resolutions on the agenda, though, addressed what had suddenly become one of the hottest topics in astronomy: what counted as a planet, and above all, whether Pluto made the cut.

Behind the controversy lay one of the most dramatic bursts of astronomical discovery since the invention of the telescope. Starting in 2002, using revolutionary new data processing technologies, astronomers had located a series of planetlike objects orbiting the Sun in the distant, frozen outer reaches of the solar system, far beyond the orbit of Pluto: Eris, Quaoar, Sedna, Haumea, and Makemake. One of them, Eris, was more massive than Pluto, and all of the new planetoids had a lot in common with Pluto—much more, arguably, than Pluto had in common with the other eight planets of the solar system.

That last was the detail that mattered to the astronomers gathered in Prague. As a planet, Pluto had always been the odd duck. The other planets have orbits around the Sun that are nearly circular, and nearly in the same plane, while Pluto's is much more elliptical, and canted at an angle of almost twenty degrees from the others. The other planets have gravitational fields that dominate the nearby regions of space, clearing away smaller bodies or locking them into orbital relationships dominated by their gravity, while Pluto's weak gravitational field has no such effect. At only 1/400th the mass of Earth, Pluto is much smaller than any of the other planets; in fact, it's smaller than some moons, including ours. In terms of its structure and composition, it has very little in common with the four rocky planets close to the Sun, and even less with the four big gas giants further out. Until the new discoveries, it had been lumped together with the planets simply because there was nothing else quite like it. The recent burst of discoveries in the outer solar system had changed that decisively.

In 1943, when astronomer Kenneth Edgeworth first predicted the existence of a belt of small icy planetoids out at the distant rim of the solar system, the technology to detect anything at that distance didn't yet exist. Advances in astronomy took a long time to catch up to Edgeworth's prediction—but catch up they did. In 1992 the first object in what had by then been named (after Gerard Kuiper, another astronomer) the Kuiper Belt was spotted, and hundreds more followed it into the textbooks as astronomers turned their attention to the frozen suburbs of the solar system. Until 2002 the largest known was about a third the size of Pluto.

The new discoveries from 2002 on made it clear that Pluto was just one more Kuiper Belt object, and its apparent uniqueness was the result of the bit of randomness that made it both large enough and close enough to the Sun to be detected much sooner than the others. That's the way the astronomers voted, too. By a substantial majority, they adopted a new definition of the word *planet* that put Pluto where it belonged, in a new class of "dwarf planets" with the former asteroid Ceres and certain other bodies, leaving the solar system with eight planets, an as yet uncounted collection of dwarf planets, and two belts of smaller objects, the asteroid belt and the Kuiper Belt.

The public reaction to this change was dramatic and almost entirely negative. Schoolchildren in particular rallied to the former planet's cause, and deluged astronomers with indignant letters demanding that poor little Pluto be restored to his former place on the roster of planets. The media proceeded to have a field day, and more often than not presented the situation as though the IAU had ganged up on Pluto in a back alley and robbed it of planetary status at gunpoint. By the time the controversy finally died down, scientists, pundits, and media personalities had talked over the fate of Pluto from every imaginable angle but one.

The omission, of course, was the astrological angle. This lapse was hardly an accident. As Richard Tarnas slyly pointed out in his pathbreaking book *Cosmos and Psyche,* astrology has exactly the same status in contemporary industrial society that Copernican astronomy had in European societies around 1600—even though it makes sense of plenty of things that the conventional wisdom can't explain, it is so unpopular as a way of understanding the universe, and so sharply at odds with the unquestioned beliefs of the age, that most educated people reject it out of hand without giving it the serious consideration it deserves.

Just as a significant number of people in Europe in 1600 ignored the conventional wisdom of their time and made the leap to the Copernican vision of a sun-centered cosmology, however, a significant number of people in the industrial world today have made a comparable leap to the astrological vision of a meaningful universe: a vision in which the placements, motions, and relationships of the solar system's major bodies have subtle linkages that connect them to everything in this corner of the cosmos, including the lives of human beings. The modern astrological community is much larger, better educated, and better funded than most people outside of it realize. Like the Copernican underground in late Renaissance Europe, the astrological community pursues and develops its distinctive vision of the cosmos in the face of the disapproval of the conventionally minded.

The vision of astrology is holistic—it recognizes the mutual connections that bind everything in the cosmos together in a common unity. It's also noetic—it recognizes the presence of consciousness and meaning in all things, not just in those anomalous lumps of meat we're pleased to call human brains. This vision has close connections to the great spiritual, mystical, and occult traditions of the world—not surprisingly, as astrology has long had an important role in many of these traditions and a central role in some. To the astrologer, furthermore, the holistic and noetic vision of the cosmos communicated by astrology isn't merely a set of abstract notions. Those who study and practice astrology know from personal experience that the movements of the planets relative to one another and the surface of the Earth do in fact correlate closely with the subtle tides that shape individual and collective consciousness—tides that can reveal glimpses of future events before they happen and can also bring happiness and success to those who know how to move in harmony with them.

In modern astrology Pluto has earned an important place. It is the planet of deep transformations, of secret and subterranean influences, of sex, death, destruction, and renewal. The sign and house it occupies in the birth chart show where secrets are kept and where drastic changes can be expected. Its aspects by transit and progression are challenging, grueling experiences with high stakes and high risks. In its personal and collective expressions, Pluto is a bear. It's also a peculiarly modern planet—a great many of its most characteristic expressions, from nuclear power to modern art, are phenomena that either did not exist or did not have their current importance until relatively recent times.

From the astrological perspective, this is no accident. Many contemporary astrologers consider the year of a planet's discovery to mark the emergence of that planet's energies into human consciousness. The discoveries of Uranus in 1781, of Neptune in 1846, and of Pluto in 1930 each marked, as this book will show, a significant shift in the collective consciousness of humanity. For that matter, there's very good reason to think that the discovery of the five classical planets in late prehistory marked an even more dramatic cascade of transformations in human consciousness and culture—the process that gave rise to history as we know it. That doesn't mean that the discovery of a planet causes the energies expressed by that planet to come into play. It means that as the influences expressed by the planet come into play, those influences affect astronomers too, and the discovery of the planet follows promptly.

This way of thinking about planetary discovery follows from the core conceptions of astrology itself. To the astrologer, human life and thought don't take place in isolation from the rest of the cosmos. Discoveries of all kinds, along with all other events of importance, do not happen at random. Rather, they reflect the great cycles of time and change that are also shown by the movements of the heavens. According to the astrological vision, in other words, the timing of Pluto's discovery—like those of the other planets before it—was written in the stars.

This implies in turn that the time of its demotion from the list of planets was equally determined by cosmic factors. According to the philosophy of astrology, as already noted, every event that takes place on earth mirrors and is mirrored by changes in the heavens. The decisions of an astronomical organization are not exempt from that law. The decision that assigned Pluto a new status, the meeting at which it took place, and the actions of each of the astronomers present in Prague that day were all part of the fabric of the universe, shaped by intersecting patterns of influence that can also be read in the heavens by those who know how to do so.

The decision of the IAU was thus as much a part of the natural unfolding of the cosmos as the discovery of Pluto had been, and it reflects a comparable watershed in the collective consciousness of our species. If this is true, as astrologers believe, then the astrological influence of Pluto—that peculiarly modern planet—was a temporary phenomenon, not a permanent one, and a great many of the characteristic expressions of Pluto's influence can be expected to lose much of their importance as the influence of the former planet fades out. As that happens, a great many of the certainties of the present time are likely to dissolve around us.

It's crucial, to make sense of what follows, not to misunderstand the core thesis of this book. I am not suggesting that Pluto was never a planet, and therefore that astrologers were wrong to take it into account in their work. Quite the contrary, I'm suggesting that from 1930 to 2006, Pluto *was* a planet, in every sense that is meaningful to astrologers. Its influence in the horoscopes and other astrological charts that were cast and interpreted during those years was just as important as astrologers thought it was, as important as that of any of the other planets. What's more, as we'll see, the influence of Pluto began to be felt in human society for roughly thirty years before it was discovered—approximately one Saturn cycle—and will continue to have an effect disproportionate to its size, though gradually declining in power, for about thirty years after its relegation to the status of dwarf planet.

After that, it will have roughly the same influence on horoscopes and other astrological charts as the other members of the category of dwarf planets—as significant, say, as Ceres. In other words, there will still be a place for it in astrology, just as there's a place for the larger asteroids, Kuiper Belt objects, and other small bodies. The only difference is that it will no longer be the potent force that it was during the Plutonian era, the period when it functioned astrologically as a planet.

It's also crucial in this context to recall that Pluto's case is not unique. The planets Uranus and Neptune, which were both discovered in modern times, show how planetary influences can emerge from the celestial backdrop, but there are other bodies that traced out both ends of Pluto's trajectory through time. Ceres, the dwarf planet just mentioned, had a similar career as a planet between 1801 and the 1850s. While astrology was at a relatively low ebb just then, and astrologers at that time apparently didn't get around to putting Ceres in the horoscopes they cast, the collective consciousness of the Cerean era—the period beginning roughly thirty years before Ceres was discovered and ending about thirty years after its demotion—showed the same sort of influence by a distinct celestial factor that the history of the Plutonian era shows so clearly.

A parallel process, though one that never quite reached the intensity of the Cerean and Plutonian eras, can be traced in the rise and fall of astronomical bodies that had a theoretical or notional reality among scientists or astrologers, but never quite managed to make it all the way into physical existence. The nonexistent planet Vulcan, between the orbit of Mercury and the Sun, and the mythical dark moon Lilith, orbiting the Earth out beyond the one moon we've actually got, both show the same kind of effects that preceded the discoveries of Ceres and Pluto, and followed their demotion. The difference was that the influences on collective consciousness represented by Vulcan and Lilith never quite managed to constellate themselves fully in the world of human experience. Vulcan had its day, attained the status of a planet for a few years, and then vanished when its existence was disproved. Lilith hovers like a phantom of the heavens, its existence accepted by a few astrologers today and rejected or ignored by everyone else. Both are still studied by some astrologers, but as we'll see, they correspond to collective dreams of our species that never quite became real.

These examples from the past offer important guidance for the future. As we will see, the core nature of Pluto can be summed up straightforwardly as *opposition to cosmos*. The ancient Greek concept of *cosmos*—literally "that which is beautifully ordered"—lies at the heart not only of astrology but of most of the world's traditions of spiritual philosophy and practice. The vision of the universe as a beautifully ordered whole, in which anything that affects one part affects all parts, in which everything has a place and nothing ever goes "away," pervades the higher possibilities of human consciousness, and is reflected in a great many mystical, religious, and occult traditions from around the world.

During the Plutonian era, that vision was in eclipse. Even those who gave it lip service routinely behaved as though their actions had no consequences and their responsibilities to the universe stopped at the boundaries of their own egos. The end of the Plutonian era, in turn, thus marks the rebirth of cosmos, a shift back toward those ways of approaching the universe that recognize, as the Lakota language beautifully expresses it, *mitakuye oyasin*—"we are all relations." The implications of that watershed in human consciousness will occupy the last chapters of this book.

ONE

The Ancient Heavens

No one will ever know when human beings first gazed up at the turning heavens and tried to figure out what messages their movements might have to communicate to dwellers on Earth. Awe and wonder don't leave visible traces in the fossil record, nor are oral traditions among the things archaeologists can dig up when they excavate the floor of a cave or the site of a long-abandoned village. All we know for certain is that at some point far back in the forgotten past, long before the first pottery was made or the first cities rose, people who were biologically indistinguishable from today's humanity started keeping track of days, seasons, and the phases of the Moon, and relating the movements of the heavens to their own experiences of life on Earth.

Despite the abysses of time that separate that distant era from ours, a few of their records survive. Archaeologists in various corners of the world have found scraps of bone, stone, and other materials scratched with tally marks in groups of thirteen and fourteen—the number of nights the Moon is visible between its first appearance in the sky and the full Moon, or between the full Moon and the last thin crescent before it disappears. The phases of the Moon and the cycle of the seasons gave human societies around the world their oldest calendars and their oldest astrologies as well: systems of timekeeping and prognostication that watched the movements of the Sun and Moon against the constellations.

Another important testimony to these ancient studies of the heavens may be found in the handful of identifiable prehistoric observatories that have survived to the present day. Stonehenge, the great stone circle on England's Salisbury Plain, is far and away the most famous of these, and it offers enigmatic but compelling evidence about the nature of the earliest astrology known to our species. Sometime around 2900 BCE, a forgotten nation devoted millions of person-hours of hard labor to dig a circular trench and heap up the chalk inside in a bank, forming a smooth artificial horizon perfect for observing the stars, with an opening toward the midsummer sunrise to allow the cycle of the year to be measured exactly. Century after century, with long interruptions now and then, the work went on. Wooden posts were raised and moved, holes dug and filled. Eventually, around 2500 BCE, the long era of observation and experimentation came to an end, and the great gray sarsen stones and the smaller bluestones were hauled into place to establish permanent sight lines toward the heavens and create the monument familiar to modern tourists.

While speculations about the nature and purpose of Stonehenge have strayed all over the range of human imagination, extending from the ridiculous to the sublime and back again, it became clear a very long time ago that among the most significant facts of the great monument was its orientation to the heavens. Back in 1740 the first serious study of Stonehenge by the pioneer archaeologist Rev. William Stukeley pointed out that the axis of the monument points straight to the place on the horizon where the Sun rises on Midsummer Day. Other alignments were spotted after Stukeley's time, but it took modern computer technology to show just how precisely the great stones were oriented toward specific features of the heavens.

That analysis was carried out by an American professor, Gerald S. Hawkins, and published in his famous 1965 book, *Stonehenge Decoded*. It showed that the great stones of the monument allowed every significant position of the Sun and Moon—sunrises and sunsets at the solstices and equinoxes, and moonrises and moonsets at the most important points of the Moon's more intricate cycles—to be tracked easily without any other equipment at all. What was more, a set of holes around the inside of the great chalk bank functioned as an extremely efficient calculator for predicting solar and lunar eclipses.

Since then, many other scholars have used similar methods to analyze the stones and sighting lines of Stonehenge and proposed different ways in which they could be used to track the movements of the Sun and Moon relative to the Earth. Some of them have looked into the possibility that Stonehenge might also have been used to track the movements of the planets and found no planetary alignments at all. For that matter, the notched stones and bones found scattered in prehistoric sites around the world have markings that correspond to the cycles of the Sun and Moon, not to any of the five visible planets.

The Sun, the Moon, and the glittering background of stars: at Stonehenge and elsewhere in the prehistoric world, these were the heavenly phenomena that people watched. There is a straightforward explanation for this. Until prehistory gave way to history, nobody seems to have noticed that there was anything special about five bright stars that changed their positions from night to night. The planets had not yet been discovered.

THE OLDEST ASTROLOGY

Some sense of what ancient peoples might have learned from their careful observations of the Sun and Moon can be found in the poem *Works and Days* by Hesiod, one of the earliest poets whose work has survived to the present day. Hesiod lived sometime in the late eighth century BCE in Boeotia, traditionally one of the most old-fashioned and conservative parts of Greece. While other parts of the world had already seen the heavens expand dramatically by his time, Hesiod passed on a traditional wisdom in his poem, a wisdom that likely dates back centuries or millennia before his time. To him, the Sun, the Moon, and the stars were all that mattered in the heavens.

Works and Days recounts the cycle of the Boeotian year, the works to be done, and the days in which to do them. In an age before written calendars, the movements of the Sun relative to the background of stars and the changes of natural phenomena on Earth were the markers that tracked the changing seasons. Plowing begins when the Pleiades set just after the Sun, harvest comes when they rise just before dawn. The rising of Arcturus at sunset heralds the approach of spring; the setting of Orion after sunset warns that storms will close the sea lanes—there's a great deal of such practical lore in Hesiod, along with such homelier and more terrestrial signs as the first appearance of snails in the spring.

Yet he also passes on another set of lore, a list of fortunate and unfortunate days marked by the Moon. What we now call a month, in those days, ran from one new moon to the next, or more precisely from the night the first thin crescent of the Moon was sighted low in the west after sunset to the night that the last thin crescent was seen low in the east, just before dawn. Days ran from sunset to sunset, and each day was numbered, from the first (the day the new moon was first seen) to the twenty-seventh or twenty-eighth (the day the old moon was last seen), with a few days in between when the Moon was not visible at all.

Each of the numbered days had a fortunate or unfortunate quality and was beneficial for some things and not for others. The first, fourth, and seventh days of each Moon, Hesiod tells us, are suitable for making offerings to the gods and goddesses; the eighth, ninth, eleventh, and twelfth are fortunate for work—the twelfth in particular is the proper day for women to set up their looms for weaving. The fifth day is ill-omened, and so is the twentieth. The sixth and twenty-first bring good fortune to a boy born on that day, but misfortune to a girl, and neither day is good for planting, and so on.

Lists of the good and bad fortune associated with each day of the Moon are anything but unique to Hesiod's poem. Another example is found in the famous Coligny calendar. This survives on the fragments of a cast bronze plaque, which was created in one of the kingdoms of ancient Gaul before that land was conquered by the Romans under

Julius Caesar. The Coligny calendar, like many other ancient calendars, defines each month by the cycles of the Moon, and inserts two additional months every five years to keep the calendar in harmony with the seasons. Each month, and each day of each month, has a specific quality of good or bad fortune, and the festivals of the Celtic year were marked on it. The calendar apparently remained in use until the coming of Christianity, when it was broken and buried.

Another related system may be found in the mansions of the Moon, a system of twenty-eight sections of the heavens through which the Moon moves, which played an important role in later Arabic and Hindu astrology. Each mansion is roughly the region of stars through which the Moon can be expected to travel in a single day and night, and each is fortunate for some things and unfortunate in others. For example, the first mansion, called Al-Sharatain in Arabic astrological writings, extends from the beginning of the astrological sign Aries to 12° Aries 51'. It is fortunate for beginning journeys and for making medicines, but unfortunate for marriage and friendship.

Similar lists can be found in the ancient Hindu scriptures, as well as in many other sources. In fragmentary form, in fact, they still appeared in almanacs in early-modern England and America. These are the last remnants, reduced by time to not much more than newspaper-horoscope simplicity, of what may well be humanity's oldest surviving astrology—older than writing, older than our knowledge of the planets, older than the geometry central to classical astrology, relying solely on counting the phases of the Moon and tracking the movement of the Sun against the vast backdrop of the stars. From the tantalizing scraps that remain, it's impossible to know just how the ancient pre-planetary astrology worked, but one thing about it can be known: a great deal of its lore and practice was passed down from teacher to student in the form of myths.

This follows from the nature of nonliterate societies. The trained human memory is a much more powerful tool for information storage than most people realize nowadays, but it has its limits, and one of the most important of those limits is the fact that it remembers some things better than others. Colorful stories told or sung in poetic verse stick in the memory better than almost anything else—see how many of the Mother Goose rhymes and children's songs you grew up with you still remember word for word! For that reason, the most effective way to prepare knowledge for long-term storage in memory is to turn the things to be memorized into the characters in a tale, then turn the tale into a poem that can be recited to children and learned by heart. In their deservedly famous book *Hamlet's Mill,* Giorgio de Santillana and Hertha von Dechend have showed that a vast range of myths and legends from around the world encode astronomical and astrological information. Most of their examples come from a later era of astrology, but here and there it's possible to glimpse the traces of ancient shamans telling stories at night and gesturing at the sky, where the characters in those stories went through their perpetual movements.

If de Santillana and von Dechend are correct—and they gathered an immense body of data to support this claim—even the earliest strata of astronomical myth include references to a cycle far greater than the ordinary movements of Sun and Moon. Track the solstices and equinoxes using an observatory such as Stonehenge, keep track of which stars rise just before the Sun and set just after him, and within a few lifetimes it becomes impossible to miss the fact that the stars themselves are shifting relative to the stations of the solar year. That shift is caused by the precession of the equinoxes, a slow wobble of the Earth's axis that takes 25,920 years to complete its cycle. The data assembled in *Hamlet's Mill* suggests that this had been at least roughly worked out in very ancient times, and the shamans and priestesses who watched the heavens from Stonehenge and its many ancient equivalents thus could fit the cycles of Moon and Sun into a truly impressive sweep of cosmic time.

Little more can be known for sure about this oldest form of astrology, the archaic star lore that can be glimpsed in its twilight years here and there as history dawns. From an astrological point of view, however, we can say one thing about it: many of the factors that play important roles in our lives today—the factors that astrologers assign to the planets—were not yet part of astrology.

This was not accidental. During the era when the archaic pre-planetary astrology spread across the world, those factors were also absent from human experience. In an age before cities, before agriculture, before governments, before writing, before countless other things that have since become ordinary parts of our existence, the range of human possibility was considerably smaller—small enough, in fact, that it makes perfect sense that the astrology of that age needed no more than the two great luminaries and the stars. Only with the immense transformations that started ten thousand years ago did a more complex palette of possibilities open up for our species—and just as that happened, for the first time in recorded history, the five visible planets came into view.

THE GREAT TRANSFORMATION

It was the most dramatic change our species has yet experienced, far more dramatic than the industrial revolution of the eighteenth century or the computer revolution of the twentieth. For at least half a million years human beings biologically identical to you and me lived in small tribal groups, made tools of stone, lived in simple huts or beneath the open sky, governed themselves, and worshiped the spirit world according to tradition and the guidance of tribal elders, and supported themselves by hunting, gathering, and occasional bouts of gardening. Then, starting around the year 8000 BCE, across a wide swath of southern Eurasia and spreading out from there, all that changed forever.

Archaeologists have named the great transformation that began in those years the Neolithic Revolution. Over a period of centuries, simple camps of hunters and gatherers were replaced first by settled villages and then by walled cities. The authority of tribal elders gave way to organized priesthoods, on the one hand, and warlords and their armies on the other. A galaxy of new arts, crafts, and technologies emerged, making life far more complex than it had ever been before, and creating scores of new occupations. Finally, sometime after these other changes, the invention of hieroglyphic writing systems transformed human life by increasing the available knowledge base exponentially, allowing human beings for the first time to record their thoughts in a form that could be passed down across the generations unchanged, without having to reshape knowledge into mythological narratives suitable for rote memorization.

It used to be popular, when these transformations were discussed in modern times, to praise them as the great achievements that kickstarted the grand march of progress that, at least in theory, would someday take us to the stars. These days, as more and more people have begun to ask where the grand march of progress is leading and whether any sane person would want to go there, it's become just as popular to mourn these same transformations as the fatal mistakes that launched our species on a collective march toward the abyss. Both these views are profoundly one-sided, of course. A less simplistic assessment of the great leap to civilization recognizes the triumphs and the tragedies, the extraordinary human achievements, and the appalling human suffering that the Neolithic Revolution and its attendant changes brought about. From this broader perspective, it becomes possible to grasp another dimension of the transformation—an astrological dimension.

The fact of the matter is that the emergence of urban societies seems to have occurred at the same time, and in the same part of the world, as the discovery of the five visible planets of the solar system: Mercury, Venus, Mars, Jupiter, and Saturn. We have no direct evidence linking these two events, to be sure, but the indirect evidence is compelling—the oldest records of planetary movements that anyone has yet discovered are from ancient Sumer, in what is now southern Iraq, where the first literate civilization known to history rose and fell some five thousand years ago.

Sumer in those days was a land of independent city-states spread out along the southern end of the shared valley of the Tigris and

Euphrates Rivers, just north of the Persian Gulf. There, as soon as the great transformation had run its course, cities protected by mud-brick walls loomed over green riverside fields of barley and brown desert lands beyond, where goats grazed. At the heart of each city rose an artificial mountain of mud brick—the Babylonians, who ruled the same land many centuries later and adopted the traditions of Sumer, called these structures *ziggurats,* from a word meaning "to build high." Each ziggurat was topped with a temple of the city's patron god or goddess, and from the steps of the temple, astronomer-priests kept careful watch on the skies and noted down every change they observed with reed pens on clay tablets.

We know a great deal about their planetary knowledge because they wrote so much of it down, and because baked-clay tablets endure for millennia in the dry climate of the Middle East. The Babylonians, the Assyrians, and other later civilizations helped that along by eagerly collecting every scrap of ancient Sumer's star lore that they could find, leaving behind whole libraries to be found by archaeologists in the nineteenth and twentieth centuries. Among the things that can be found in these libraries are detailed accounts of the movements of planets dating back many thousands of years, along with formulas for predicting the movements of the planets and the timing of solar and lunar eclipses. The raw data needed to work out those formulas must have taken many centuries to record and correlate, especially when it's remembered that the people responsible for these records had no telescopes or clocks, just their own eyes and the measure of time provided by the turning heavens and the changing seasons.

Another data point is worth mentioning here. The Sumerian names for the five visible planets are not, in fact, in the Sumerian language. Just as our own language borrowed its names for those same five planets from the Latin language, which was many centuries older than English, the Sumerians borrowed some of their planet names from an older language of which no other trace apparently survives: Sagmegar for Jupiter, Dilbat for Venus, and Salbatanu for Mars are not Sumerian words and nobody knows what they originally meant. The Sumerians were not the first urban society in the Middle East, just the first to work out the trick of writing so that they could leave records we can interpret today. It therefore seems to have been one of those earlier Middle Eastern societies, urban (or proto-urban) but not yet literate, that first noticed that five bright stars weren't fixed in place the way the others were but moved slowly across the panoply of the sky, following roughly the same track through the stars that the Sun marked out over the course of the year.

According to astrology, as mentioned in this book's introduction, so momentous a discovery must have had tremendous implications in terms of every aspect of human life. The testimony of archaeology suggests that this was, in fact, the case—that the great transformation of human history that brought civilization into being, and the discovery of five moving lights in the heavens distinct from the fixed stars, were intimately connected.

THE COMING OF THE PLANETS

The points just made can be put into their deeper perspective by remembering a detail of astrological lore. The things that set apart the Sumerians and the other early civilizations of the Middle East from other peoples of their time—the things that made them different from every other human society that had ever existed until that point—*were precisely the things that astrology assigns to the five visible planets.* Saturn, according to astrological tradition, governs agriculture and all enduring things, such as permanent settlements. Jupiter governs organized religion, priesthoods, and temples. Mars governs war and also animal herding. Venus governs all the arts and crafts that flowered so spectacularly in the early civilizations, as well as gardening. Mercury governs technology, trade, occult sciences such as magic and astrology, and the crucial invention of writing.

In these traditional correspondences, we can catch the fading echoes of the first great age of astrological discovery, a forgotten intellectual revolution more than five millennia in the past, during which students of the skies first began to glimpse powers no one had recognized before them and started to figure out how those powers helped to shape human destiny. As mentioned in the introduction, it's a widely held theory among today's astrologers that the discovery of a new planet corresponds to the awakening of a new influence in the collective consciousness of our species. By observing the effects that correlate to planetary discoveries during recorded history it's possible to guess something of what it must have been like to be present in those distant years, when the influences of five newly discovered worlds stirred human consciousness for the first time and made the world forever different.

The details of discovery are of course long lost, but archaeological and astronomical data converge to suggest a plausible order in which it may have happened. Venus is far and away the brightest object in the sky other than the Sun and Moon, and its appearances as the evening and morning star are striking enough to catch the attention of any skywatcher. In some ancient societies—Greece in Hesiod's time is one example—the morning and evening star were thought to be two different things, but if an enterprising astrologer keeping watch at dawn and dusk happened to track the movements of these two bright objects, making notches on a stick to count the days between their appearances, their identity would not have been hard to grasp.

Once the astrologers of that time realized that Venus was a single moving object, started keeping track of its wanderings through the sky, and realized that it had its own potent influences on human life, the hunt for others would soon have begun, and it probably would not have taken long for Mars, Jupiter, and Saturn to be spotted. All three are relatively large and bright when compared to the stars, and their movements can be tracked readily enough in a fairly short time if the nights are clear (as they so often are in the Middle East). Mercury is a tougher task, since it never strays more than a short distance from the Sun. Careful observation at sunset and dawn over a long period, perhaps stretching over many centuries, would have been needed to notice the bright little star that appears for a few days at long intervals, just before dawn and just after sunset in alternation.

Compare this astronomical data to the archaeological record and a fascinating pattern emerges. The first things to happen as the earliest Middle Eastern civilizations emerged out of the tribal communities that preceded them was that existing crafts such as pottery and weaving became far more common and elaborate than they had been, new crafts emerged, and mixed-crop gardens first began to supplement, and then to replace, the traditional diet of wild game and wild plants. The resulting village societies seem to have settled into a stable pattern for some centuries. Then, over a fairly short time, walled cities, monumental architecture, religious shrines, large-scale grain agriculture, and animal herding all show up, and the first signs of organized warfare and social hierarchy start to appear. Later—many centuries later, as Sumer was born—writing, bronze tools, magic as a study and practice separate from religion, and such technological achievements as the wheeled oxcart arrive. Just as the relative visibility of the planets would suggest, the influence of Venus came first, then those of Mars, Jupiter, and Saturn, and finally that of Mercury.

The ways that astrology was practiced during that era of shattering transformation are of course long forgotten. A likely guess—though it really is no more than a guess—is that most of the astrologers of the era continued with the old day-counting astrology of Sun, Moon, and stars, with the newly discovered planets patched into the system in an ad hoc manner, interpreted in various ways by different traditions. Mythic narratives of the sort that had stored up the legacy of pre-planetary astrology certainly had a similar role in this proto-planetary astrology. This is shown by the great majority of the myths and legends that de Santillana and von Dechend discussed in *Hamlet's Mill,* which derive from the era when the planets had become significant factors, but constellations outside the zodiac still had an important role in astrology and the mathematics and geometry of planetary movement, the basis for later astrological traditions, had not yet been worked out.

Every night, if this hypothesis is correct, the astrologer-priests of that distant time would have kept watch to see which stars set just after sunset and rose just before sunrise and followed the phases of the Moon just as their ancestors had done. In addition, though, they would watch the movements of the planets across the constellations. By comparing these movements with the motions of Sun and Moon against that same backdrop they will have been able to make the first shrewd guesses about what those movements meant. Over time, the clay tablet records of planetary movements and events on Earth mounted up, the guesses became more exact, the astrologer-priests became more influential, and the historically attested astrology of Sumer and Babylon gradually emerged.

One odd feature of that astrology has remained fixed in place ever since: the idea that the celestial influences raying down on the Earth can be understood as a set of seven. The Sun, the Moon, and the five visible planets were of course made into such a set, and assigned to the days of the week, that legacy of ancient Mesopotamian astrology found today on every wall calendar. Traditional as it is, the habit of counting the Sun and Moon among the planets poses as many questions as it solves. Astrologers in those times already recognized that the influences of the Sun and Moon—the luminaries as distinct from the planets— belong to a different category than those of the planets, being at once stronger and broader in their effects. Yet the idea of a sevenfold pattern of forces is very deeply rooted in the human psyche and is echoed in esoteric spiritual traditions from around the world.

Another dimension of this ancient astrology less well reflected in the later forms of the art has to do with the kind of information the old astrologers extracted from the skies. To judge from the earliest surviving astrological records, the astrologer-priests of the Tigris and Euphrates valleys thought that astrology was mostly about politics. They watched the movements of the heavens and compared them to the rise and fall of kingdoms on the Earth, and gradually learned to anticipate the latter by observing the former. That branch of astrology still exists. It is called mundane astrology, from the Latin word *mundus,* "world," and the techniques of the modern mundane astrologer still echo those used in Sumer five thousand years ago.

Individual birth charts played only an incidental role in the astrology of the proto-planetary era. The birth of a new prince or princess would of course be noted as a politically important event, and the planetary positions at that time considered. Still, the predictions of individual personality and psychology that today's astrologers draw from a birth chart were of little interest to their ancient equivalents, who mostly wanted to know whether the child would live or die and whether its birth indicated good or bad fortune for the city-state it might grow up to rule. It took important transformations in Mesopotamian culture, followed by the arrival of a new cultural impetus from outside the valleys of the Tigris and the Euphrates, to transform this approach to the first drafts of the astrology we know today.

THE BIRTH OF CLASSICAL ASTROLOGY

The Babylonians, whose civilization rose in the Tigris-Euphrates valley a millennium after Sumer's heyday, were much more skilled at mathematics than the Sumerians or, for that matter, any other known culture from before their time. They used a mathematical system based on the number sixty and its multiples, a system that shaped the oldest versions of our mathematics, which is why—even though our number system is based on multiples of ten rather than of sixty—we still count sixty minutes in every hour and 360 degrees in every circle. As they observed the stars and studied the clay tablet records of their ancestors, Babylonian astrologers worked out mathematical formulae to track the movements of the Sun, Moon, and planets to a fine degree of precision. Using those formulae, they could calculate horoscopes from the distant past and the far future. By the sixth century BCE, they had also begun to refocus their attention away from strictly political concerns and had begun specializing in casting and interpreting individual birth charts, the keynote of the later astrological tradition.

Even so, it was the ancient Greeks, with their passion for logic and mathematics, who took the astrological discoveries of the Babylonians and developed them into classical astrology. After Alexander the Great's armies conquered the Tigris and Euphrates valleys in 331 BCE, the ancient star lore of Sumer and Babylon provided new grist for the mills of Greek mathematics and philosophy, and the astrology that emerged from this fusion was directly ancestral to the kind most astrologers in the Western world practice today.

The great contribution the Greeks made to astrology was geometrical. They seem to have been the first to realize that certain angles made between planets, when seen from Earth, announce certain distinct relationships between the influences of those planets. Today, astrologers call those angles "aspects," and assign to them the same meaning that the astrologers of ancient Greece did. The Greeks also finished the process of dividing the ecliptic—the narrow band of sky along which the Sun, Moon, and planets move—into twelve equal sections, each covering an arc of 30°, counting around the circle of the ecliptic from the point at which the Sun crosses the celestial equator in spring. These are the familiar signs of the zodiac—these are not the same as the constellations, a point too often missed by beginners.*

Finally, the Greeks noticed that certain sections of sky also affected the way that the Sun, Moon, and planets influenced the details of human life, and that these sections—unlike the signs of the zodiac—varied from person to person and from place to place. Many centuries of study and experiment were needed to move from this basic insight to the system of twelve houses used by today's astrologers. Even today, astrologers differ concerning the best way to locate the cusps (dividing lines) of the houses in the heavens, and no doubt many more centuries of close observation will be needed to come to a consensus on that issue.

---

*Confusing the two is also a common mistake of would-be skeptics who generally don't bother to learn much about the things that they denounce. The confusion comes because the signs still take their names from the constellations that originally occupied them when the Greek astrologers went to work.

Since astrology is based on evidence rather than theory, there is no other way to work things out.

The placement of planets in houses determine what things the planets affect in each person's life, and the placement of planets in signs determine the quality or "flavor" the planets will have in each person's life and chart. Within these paired frameworks, however, the seven planets—more precisely, the two luminaries, Sun and Moon, and the five planets properly so called—were the powerhouses of the heavens in classical astrology. Philosophers and astrologers came to see the sevenfold order defined by these celestial lights in everything on Earth. The seven days of the week were assigned to the luminaries and the planets; so were herbs, stones, animals, personality types, periods of the human lifespan, and much more. For generation after generation, people took this sevenfold order for granted. It became the foundation of much of ancient, medieval, and Renaissance thought. Over a span of more than four thousand years, from the time of Sumer until the dawn of the Industrial Revolution, it seemed obvious to everyone that there had to be seven and only seven primary astrological powers in the sky. Thus, it's easy to imagine the shockwaves that spread through the educated world when it suddenly turned out there were more planets than the five that had been known to the ancients. Those newly discovered planets, in turn, also marked the emergence of new forces in human life and thought—forces that we are still struggling to integrate in ourselves and our societies today.

TWO

Two New Worlds

William Herschel was puzzled. One of the most respected astronomers in eighteenth-century Britain, the designer and builder of a new reflecting telescope that the assembled experts at Greenwich Observatory unanimously described as the best they had ever seen, he was staring through the eyepiece of that very telescope at a field of stars on the night of March 13, 1781. That was nothing unusual for a man who spent most clear evenings exploring the heavens. What baffled him that night was that one of the stars he was looking at appeared to be slightly larger than the others, and that was impossible.

He knew, as we know today, that the stars are so far away from Earth that no telescope on Earth's surface can possibly show a star as anything but a single point of light. Nonetheless, the star he was observing appeared to be a very small disk. Sure that this had to be some kind of illusion, he swapped out the eyepiece he was using for another with double the magnification. When he did so, however, the disk expanded visibly. Another eyepiece of even greater power produced another expansion.

What was the object, then? It looked like a planet, but like everyone else in eighteenth-century Europe, Herschel knew perfectly well that there were five and only five planets. He finally decided that the strange object was probably a comet and noted down its position carefully before turning his telescope to other parts of the heavens.

Over the days that followed, though, he told his fellow astronomers about the object he'd seen. They turned their telescopes toward it and noted that it didn't look or behave like a comet. It moved slowly and steadily across the background of stars the way planets did, though at half the pace of Saturn, the slowest planet then known. It was also a bright lustrous disk without any of the cloudiness that marks comets—the result, as we now know, of dust and gases boiling off into space from the comet's surface, to be swept away by the solar wind and form the comet's tail. Day by day, as Herschel and his colleagues compared notes, it became harder to avoid the realization that the utterly unbelievable had happened: the object Herschel had sighted really was a sixth planet unknown to the ancients.

One obvious question was what to call the new planet. Herschel himself, in a burst of patriotism, wanted to call it *Georgium Sidus,* the Star of George, after King George III of England. Others suggested simply calling it Herschel after its discoverer, and this caught on for a while. Eventually, though, tradition triumphed, and the new planet was given a name out of classical mythology like those of the other planets: Uranus, after the primeval god of the sky, mate of the earth-mother Gaia and father of Saturn.

Another issue of more immediate importance was tracking the new planet's orbit. Careful measurements of the movements of Uranus allowed astronomers to work that out in some detail, and the quest for more data sent researchers digging back through old observatory records in the hope of finding earlier sightings of the newly discovered world. It turned out that several other astronomers had spotted Uranus before Herschel did, but none of them had noticed that it wasn't just another star. Those sightings immediately raised another difficulty for astronomers, however, because those sightings didn't place Uranus quite where calculations of Uranus's orbit based on Herschel's sightings said it should have been.

That was an issue of immense importance in Herschel's time. Nearly a century before the discovery of Uranus, Isaac Newton had solved some of the greatest riddles of astronomy by working out the laws of gravity mathematically and showing that they explained the observed movements of the Sun, the Moon, and the five planets then known. Newton's work had revolutionized astronomy, giving astronomers a toolkit of powerful mathematical methods for projecting planetary orbits forward and back in time. If Uranus wasn't exactly where it was supposed to be, that meant either that Newton's math was wrong—an unthinkable idea in Herschel's day—or that some unknown factor was affecting Uranus, speeding up its orbit at certain times and slowing it down at others.

The obvious culprit was another planet that was further out from the Sun, and large enough that its gravitational field could have a measurable effect on the orbit of Uranus. By the early nineteenth century, as a result of the discovery of Ceres (described later on in chapter 3), the possibility of finding new planets was on many astronomers' minds. That led two experts—the English mathematician John Couch Adams and the French astronomer Urbain Le Verrier—to tackle the immense challenge of trying to find the position of the unknown planet, using the clues provided by the vagaries of Uranus's motion.

By 1845, working unknown to each other, both men had succeeded in calculating the likely location of the planet that was disrupting Uranus's movements. The next problem was getting astronomers to look there—an issue that in both cases, prophetically enough, turned into an absurd chapter of unexpected mistakes and strange confusions. Finally, Le Verrier won the race. A colleague of his at the Berlin Observatory, Johann Gottfried Galle, took the French savant's best estimate of the unknown planet's position and pointed a telescope in the right direction. On the night of September 23, 1846, he found himself staring at a tiny blue disk less than a degree from the place where Le Verrier asked him to look.

Le Verrier tried to get the planet named after him, but once again tradition prevailed. On account of its striking blue color, the new planet was named Neptune, after the Roman god of the sea. In a mere sixty-five years, the solar system had grown dramatically, reaching millions of miles farther out into space, and including seven planets rather than the classical five.

URANUS AND NEPTUNE IN ASTROLOGY

Astrology was at a very low ebb in 1781 when William Herschel made his unexpected discovery. The dogmatic materialism of the age of reason had combined with other broad shifts in intellectual fashions to make the ancient science of the stars not merely unpopular but largely forgotten in most of Europe. Only in England did it survive as a living tradition. That survival hinged on an improbable series of events that played out more than a century before Uranus appeared in the field of view of Herschel's telescope.

In 1641 the English Civil War broke out, pitting the Royalist armies of King Charles I against Parliamentarian rebels. Until that time, publishers in England labored under strict political and religious censorship, but war broke the grip of the Crown and the Church of England on London's printing industry and made it possible to publish books on a range of previously forbidden subjects, including astrology.

One astrologer in particular took advantage of the newfound freedom. William Lilly was a widely respected professional astrologer. He was also a strong supporter of the Parliamentary cause and predicted in a series of pamphlets and almanacs that Parliament would triumph and King Charles would die a violent death. He turned out to be right on both counts, and in 1647, in the wake of the Parliamentary victory, he published a comprehensive textbook of astrology, *Christian Astrology.** What set this book apart from every other book on astrology that had been published up to that time is simply that it was written entirely in English.

---

*The title was meant to reassure potential readers who were uncertain about astrology's religious bona fides.

All throughout Europe, Latin was the language of the educated, and astrological textbooks had inevitably been written in that language. Outside England, as a result, the shift in intellectual fashions that made astrology unpopular among the cultured meant that those members of the less educated, lower classes who might otherwise have continued to practice it couldn't learn it from the available manuals. In England, by contrast, Lilly's textbook—and dozens of other English-language astrological publications that followed it—saw to it that astrology could take refuge among country wise-women and cunning men, who knew not a word of Latin but could work their way through Lilly's easy-to-use instructions.

By the time Uranus was discovered, as a result, astrology was all but extinct in most European countries but survived in a quiet way in England, supported by a steady stream of publications that took advantage of England's continued freedom of the press. Two years after Herschel's discovery, for example, the astrologer Ebenezer Sibley published *Illustrations of Astrology,* a handbook of the art that also included a spirited defense of its relevance. Two years further on, in 1786, an anonymous astrologer using the pseudonym "C. Heydon" published *The New Astrologer,* a concise manual teaching beginning students how to cast and interpret astrological charts. Neither book covers the movements and meanings of Uranus, but one or both of them would have been in the libraries of the astrologers who, within a few years of the new planet's discovery, began trying to figure out how to fit it into the astrological heavens.

Curiously, this isn't what you'll read if you consult histories of astrology written by historians who aren't astrologers. Many of these have claimed that the discovery of Uranus dealt a terrible blow to the few astrologers who were still active in the late eighteenth and early nineteenth centuries. That's what modern skeptics like to think, no doubt, but it's not what the evidence says. On the contrary, the new planet became a subject of immediate interest among astrologers, who began almost at once to try to figure out what influence the new planet brought to bear on human affairs. Their tools were the same ones that their predecessors in the Tigris and Euphrates valleys had used more than four millennia earlier: careful examination of the planet's position and aspects in a multitude of astrological charts.

By 1830 this process was far enough along that the astrologer Richard Morrison was confident enough to publish predictions concerning a conjunction of Mars and Uranus in 18° Aquarius in April of the following year. Morrison was among the most influential astrologers in England at that time. Under the pen name "Zadkiel," he published an annual astrological almanac and a great many other publications on the interpretation of the stars. His predictions—increased mortality, sharp fluctuations in the financial markets, and political troubles in Britain—would not be out of place in an astrological book written today, for the basic character of Uranus had already been worked out by his time. The predictions also turned out to be quite correct.

Uranus, according to astrologers then and now, is the planet of individuality, eccentricity, and radical change. Its position in your natal chart shows what part of your personality is going to be quirky and unexpected, and the aspects it makes by transit and progression warn you when part of your life is going to be turned upside down. The more strongly placed it is in your chart, the more eccentric you will be. On a broader scale, it's associated with political revolutions, natural disasters, and dramatic historical transformations. All this was worked out less than fifty years after the discovery of the new planet.

It's worth noting that while the older planets show obvious connections between the gods for whom they are named and the astrological influences they exert, Uranus does not. Nothing in the mythology of the god Uranus, the old Greek sky-father, has any particular resonance with the way that the planet Uranus affects astrological charts. The reason for the difference is quite simple: Uranus was not named by astrologers. The Sumerian astrologer-priests who gave the five classical planets the names of deities evidently made the assignment on the basis of their knowledge of the planets' influence on Earth. The astronomers

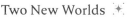

who named Uranus, of course, did no such thing. That said, it's by no means entirely inappropriate that a planet as quirky as Uranus would have a name that gives no warning of its effect!

By the time Neptune was discovered in 1846, accordingly, astrologers already had a fair amount of practice in the ancient art of figuring out the effects of a newly discovered planet, and they went to work on the newcomer almost immediately. By that time, astrology had begun to shake off the weight of its long era of unpopularity, and manuals of astrology could be found in nearly every European language. Though casting horoscopes for pay was still legally prohibited in most Western countries, that law was mostly honored in the breach. Astrological books, magazines, and almanacs commanded steady sales. In such an environment, the discovery of a new planet was guaranteed to attract the attention of astrologers.

Even so, most astrologers at the time took a cautious approach to the interpretation of Neptune. The great Alan Leo (William Frederick Allan), one of the two or three most widely respected astrologers in the world at the beginning of the twentieth century, wrote in his 1904 textbook *How to Judge a Nativity:* "Many years must elapse before sufficient tabulation is made to warrant a reliable opinion concerning Neptune's vibrations." Even today, many astrologers are careful about specifying the limits of Neptune's influence.

One very important reason for that caution is the nature of the Neptunian influence itself. As astrologers tracked the position of the new planet in the horoscopes they cast, they discovered that they were dealing with a force as different from that of Uranus as they could imagine. Where Uranus was brash, irrepressible, revolutionary, uncompromising, Neptune was subtle, elusive, pervasive, indeterminate. Its influence showed itself in dreams and fancies, confusion and self-deception, and trance and other alternative states of consciousness: every place, in fact, where the individuality indicated by Uranus fades out into a larger whole. The strange mistakes and confusions that had hindered the discovery of Neptune turned out to be typical of the planet itself, or rather of what usually happens when people try to pin down so elusive and evasive an influence.

In its most general terms, Neptune might best be characterized as the planet of unity and impersonality, of the dissolution of individual boundaries into whole systems. Its position in your natal chart shows where your personality flows most directly into the impersonal. The aspects it makes to your chart by transit or progression warn you when part of your life is going to be subject to influences you will not be able to understand. The more strongly placed it is in your chart, the more strongly your personality and your life will be shaped by forces rooted in the transcendent, or in the collective life of your time. In its highest expressions, its effect can take the form of profound creative inspiration, religious experience, or humanitarian effort; in its mid-level manifestations, it tells you where your dreams and daydreams dwell; while in its most degraded forms, it becomes the nexus of deception and self-deception, self-defeating behaviors, alcoholism, drug abuse, and madness.

None of these things are characteristic of the Roman god Neptune, for whom the new planet was named. Once again, the planet was not named by astrologers. It was given its name by astronomers, who noticed its blue color and on that basis gave it the name of the old god of the sea. There is, nonetheless, a certain symbolic appropriateness in the name, for the planet Neptune has an oceanic quality. Like the ocean, it hides what lies beneath the surface, and its tides bring unsuspected things onto the shore and then sweep them away again. The mystical experiences that are among its highest manifestations have often been called "oceanic"; the realms of madness and addiction that are among its lowest manifestations also resemble an ocean in which the personality can be swept away and drowned.

URANUS AND NEPTUNE IN HISTORY

According to the astrological theory discussed in this book's introduction, the discovery of a previously unknown planet should correlate fairly precisely in time to the emergence of a new set of influences on humanity's individual and collective existence. The discoveries of Uranus and Neptune offer good evidence for the truth of that theory, because that's exactly what happened in both these cases. As examples of the impact of astrology on history, in fact, the discoveries of Uranus and Neptune are hard to beat. Both discoveries happened at crucial watersheds in world history, and the nature of each transformation reflected the astrological influence of the newly discovered planet to a remarkable degree.

The discovery of Uranus in 1781 thus took place on the cusp of one of history's great ages of revolutionary upheaval. That same year, the American Revolution reached its decisive climax at the Battle of Yorktown, where the British military, the strongest in the world, was humbled by the ragtag American colonists and their French allies. When the British force at Yorktown marched out to surrender on October 19 of that year, their regimental bands played a tune titled "The World Turned Upside Down"—as perfect an anthem for the influence of Uranus as can be imagined. Thereafter, as the newly founded American republic adjusted to the shock of independence and hammered out its constitution, the almost unheard-of concept of the rights of the individual emerged as a central theme around which social movements would rally and battles be fought all around the world for many years to come.

That same theme exploded with Uranian force in France just eight years after the planet's discovery, when an ongoing squabble over taxes that pitted King Louis XVI against the French aristocracy forced the king to convene the French Parliament for the first time in many decades. The Parliament had three houses—one for the nobles, one for the clergy, and one for the "Third Estate," the elected representatives of the French people, who were expected to do no more than rubber-stamp the decisions of their betters. That had happened every other time the Parliament had been convened, but all those had happened before Uranus was discovered.

What happened instead in 1789 was that the representatives of the Third Estate declared themselves the National Assembly, invited sympathetic members of the nobility and clergy to join them, seized control of the government and the nation, and passed a Declaration of the Rights of Man and of the Citizen that became the template for the next century of global political activism. While the French Revolution descended thereafter into mass murder, dictatorship, and war, its aftermath saw the rise of radical movements all over Europe and the world, pushing for individual liberties that nobody had seen as political issues a few generations before.

Meanwhile the same Uranian influences were spreading in other directions. Before 1781 artists, writers, poets, and people in other creative fields were simply craftspeople, laboring at their trade in much the same spirit as potters and carpenters, without anything like the reputation for eccentricity and originality that they later attained. It was only after the discovery of Uranus that the idea of the creative artist as a uniquely inspired individual seized the collective imagination. Artists and writers were as quick to absorb those influences as anyone and began pushing the boundaries of their fields as never before. It was in the wake of the discovery of Uranus, for example, that a young Englishwoman named Mary Wollstonecraft Shelley wrote the first science fiction novel, *Frankenstein,* and the American author Edgar Allan Poe—a profoundly Uranian figure—invented the detective story with "The Murders in the Rue Morgue" and transformed the Gothic horror genre of the eighteenth century into the modern horror story with tales such as "The Pit and the Pendulum," and "The Black Cat."

As Shelley's novel suggests, Uranus is also the planet of science and technology. In the year 1781 the word *scientist* did not yet exist— people who practiced what we now call science were called "natural philosophers"—and the idea of replacing human and animal muscle with mechanical power, the keynote of the Industrial Revolution, was just beginning to find takers in Britain and a few other countries. James Watt designed the first really efficient steam engine in 1776, but it was only after 1781 that it began to transform the British economy, followed by those of the rest of the world. The world changed dramatically thereafter as steam power gave birth to the railroad, the steamship, the factory, and a galaxy of other radical innovations. As discovery followed discovery, scientific research came to be seen as a normal and useful human activity, something that many people did in their spare time—thus the Uranian theme of individualism found an important expression in the long list of hobbyist-researchers who ended up contributing immensely to the growth of scientific knowledge.

Uranus is also the planet of alternative sexualities. In the late nineteenth and early twentieth centuries, in fact, gay men used the term "Uranians" for themselves. Human beings have been having same-sex relationships since well before we finished becoming human—our closest animal relatives, the bonobos, are notorious for their omnivorous sexual appetites—but participating in such relationships was rarely seen as a matter of identity; it was just something that some people did. That changed after 1781, as the first gay and lesbian subcultures began to emerge. The Uranian theme of uniqueness, of standing apart from the crowd, made the emergence of distinctive alternative sexual identities inescapable.

All these changes were still in process when the influence of Neptune began to be felt. Neptune is also a planet of revolution, but the revolutions it brought focused not on the rights of the individual but on the rights of entire classes and other collective groups.

In 1848, three years after Neptune was discovered, Karl Marx and Friedrich Engels penned *The Communist Manifesto*—the most famous of a galaxy of radical proclamations that each claimed to herald the inevitable wave of the future, and the only one that is still remembered by anyone but a handful of historians. In that same year, revolutions broke out across most of Europe, but those uprisings could not have been more different from the decisive Uranus-inspired revolutions in America and France. The 1848 revolutions were disorganized and spontaneous; their goals were little more than empty slogans. By 1849 they had fizzled out, having terrified the ruling classes of the time but done little else.

Thomas Mann's Nobel Prize–winning 1901 novel *Buddenbrooks* catches the flavor of the Neptunian revolutionaries brilliantly. One of his characters, Johann Buddenbrook, is an official in one of the little independent German republics of the time, and he has to confront a rebellious mob during the rebellions of 1848. The mob's spokesman yells at him, "I say we wants a republic, that's what I be sayin'!" "But, you fool," Buddenbrook replies, "you've already got one." "Well, Herr Consul, then we wants another!" is the rejoinder. Such leadership does not overthrow kingdoms and establish new political institutions. For half a century following the discovery of Neptune that was the character of radical politics over much of the world: idealistic, impractical, fond of brandishing slogans, striking dramatic poses, and blowing up the occasional politician or aristocrat, but remarkably ineffective at bringing about lasting changes. It would take the arrival of a new planetary influence to change that and turn revolution back into a deadly game once again.

The same impractical idealism can be seen in another important feature of the Neptunian era, the gold rushes that swept the Western world during the half century following Neptune's discovery. Gold had been discovered countless times before 1846 without causing extraordinary popular delusions, but news of the discovery of gold in northern California in 1848 caused nearly 200,000 people to abandon their everyday lives and head for the gold country in the excited certainty that they would come home rich. A few of them succeeded; the vast majority came home as poor as ever, and quite a few of them never came home at all—disease and violence were rife in the mining camps, and overwork and exposure also accounted for their share of deaths. Yet the same thing happened when gold was discovered in Australia in 1851, in South Africa in 1886, and in the Klondike and Alaska in the 1890s—and these are only the biggest names in the litany of late nineteenth-century gold rushes.

Other creations of the Neptunian era were more constructive. As the planet that governs mass phenomena, it rules government social welfare schemes—the first of these was set up in Germany in 1883. It governs public parks—the first city park paid for out of municipal funds was established in Birkenhead, England, in 1847, and the first national park was created in the United States in 1876. It governs world's fairs, those spectacles for the masses—the first of these, the Great Exhibition, took place in London in 1851. It also governs the caring professions— Florence Nightingale's founding the modern nursing profession in 1854, less than a decade after Neptune's discovery, is a typical expression of the Neptunian era.

Neptune is also the planet of countercultures and of social and cultural experimentation. The first half of the nineteenth century was, accordingly, the great seedtime of Western countercultures, the period during which small groups of young radicals began working out what would become the standard template of alternative culture for the next two centuries and more. Anyone who thinks communes were invented in the sixties might find it useful to read American novelist Nathaniel Hawthorne's *The Blithedale Romance,* originally published in 1852, and based on Hawthorne's own experience in the early nineteenth-century Boston counterculture and his time on a Massachusetts commune in 1841. By the second half of the nineteenth century, communes and countercultures were known phenomena all over the Western world and had begun to find their way into the rest of the world, carrying Neptunian dreams with them.

Feminism was another product of the Neptunian influence. While a handful of women had protested against the mistreatment of their sex from the Middle Ages on, feminism as a significant social movement in the Western world dates from the Seneca Falls Convention of 1848—that year again!—when women who had been radicalized by the antislavery movement met to apply the same logic to the unequal status of women in the world of their time. Over the decades that followed, this first wave of feminism gradually focused its efforts on the goal of winning the vote for women.

In typically Neptunian fashion, that goal was promptly painted in the hues of extreme idealism. Since women in the Victorian mindset were naturally good and pure and gentle, it was argued, giving them the vote would inevitably lead to a more moral society. On an equally Neptunian plane, many of the women who joined the crusade to win the vote for women also directed energy into a series of moral crusades, above all the prohibition of alcoholic beverages; it's telling that the Women's Christian Temperance Union, founded in 1877, became the largest women's organization of the time, and lobbied for laws against alcohol and prostitution as well as for giving women the vote. It was only after 1900, when a different planetary influence came into play, that the decidedly prim and proper tone of early feminism gave way to something much closer to the modern sexually charged and socially radical version of the movement.

Another expression of the Neptunian influence is modern occultism. Occult arts such as magic and divination go back far into prehistory, of course. In the days before the discovery of the five visible planets, to judge from the practices of modern hunter-gatherer peoples and the equivocal traces discovered by archaeologists, it was governed by the Moon and resembled nothing so much as today's surviving shamanic traditions—Joseph Campbell's title for the magical spirituality of that distant age, "the Way of the Animal Powers," was well chosen. Egypt, that most conservative of ancient cultures, still preserved the archaic lunar connection by making Thoth, the god of learning and magic, the lord of the Moon.

With the coming of the planets, however, occultism became one of the things ruled by Mercury, the swift-moving messenger of the planetary gods. Shamanistic lore learned from elders and spirits gave way to magical tomes written on papyrus scrolls, clay tablets, and eventually books of parchment and paper. Words and names of power, intricate sigils and diagrams, and the elaborate processes of alchemy and ceremonial magic took over from the trance states and ecstatic dances of the earlier tradition.

But Mercury's rulership over occultism also gave way in due time. The occult philosophies and practices that emerged in the second half of the nineteenth century, the era of the Theosophical Society and the Hermetic Order of the Golden Dawn, were distinctively Neptunian, with a focus on visionary experience and a variety of colorful alternative histories of the world shot through with Neptunian themes. The timing is precise: the dawn of the modern occult revival can be dated to 1854, eight years after Neptune's discovery, when the French writer Alphonse Constant published the first volume of *Dogme et Rituel de la Haute Magie* (*Doctrine and Ritual of High Magic*) under the pen name that would make him famous, Eliphas Lévi. From that year to the present, occultism has had a continuing presence, and not just in the Western world—occult traditions echoing those that Lévi set in motion can be found in abundance in India and Japan, for example

As science fiction is the distinctive literature of the Uranian influence, in turn, fantasy is the distinctive literature of the Neptunian influence. Here again, the timing is exact. Nathaniel Hawthorne published his epochal *A Wonder-Book for Girls and Boys,* the first modern work of children's fantasy, in 1851. The first fantasy novel for adults, George Macdonald's *Phantastes,* appeared in 1858, and the most famous of all children's fantasy stories, Lewis Carroll's *Alice in Wonderland,* saw print in 1865. These were hallmarks of a period in which the unreal, the imaginary, and the fantastic played a greater role in the arts than ever before.

Just as the principles of astrology would suggest, in other words, the discoveries of Uranus and Neptune each marked the arrival of a major new influence in human affairs. Here again, it is important to remember that the astronomers who spotted Uranus and Neptune for the first time didn't cause those new influences to arrive. On the contrary, George Herschel and Johann Galle were as subject to astrological influences as everyone else on Earth then and now and their discoveries were just as much a part of the arrival of the new influences as the Battle of Yorktown or the penning of *The Communist Manifesto.* It would not be unreasonable to say, in fact, that Uranus and Neptune revealed themselves to these astronomers when it was time for their influences to come into play.

Yet the details of the discovery are also important, for an interesting common feature links the influences of each newly discovered planet to the place of discovery. This link isn't absolute—the effects of a planet's discovery can be traced all over the world—but it can be striking. Uranus was discovered from Great Britain, for example, and many of the social changes that followed had Great Britain as ground zero. Few countries anywhere were as profoundly shaken as Britain by the twin impacts of the American and French Revolutions, the Industrial Revolution first happened in Britain, and the emergence of gay and lesbian identities and subcultures proceeded there faster than anywhere else in Europe. In the same way, Neptune was discovered from a German observatory, and it's noteworthy that Germany was more heavily shaken by the 1848 uprisings than any other part of Europe, the authors of *The Communist Manifesto* were both Germans, and fantasy in literature and the arts became a pervasive feature of German culture during the Neptunian era, with consequences that would turn malevolent and feed into racist and national ideologies once Pluto's influence began to be felt.

Time as well as place deserves attention here. Though the full impact of the Uranian and Neptunian currents arrived only with the discovery of their respective planets, a glance back through the decades immediately beforehand shows that the influence of each planet had begun to be felt some years before the moment of discovery. Uranus is to some extent an exception to the rule, as its core themes of individual rights and political revolution surged into action very suddenly—as the astrological nature of the planet would suggest. Even so, to cite an obvious example, the American Revolution didn't begin in 1781; it started in 1775, and the pressures that made it inevitable had been building steadily for a decade before the first rattle of musketry sounded at Concord Bridge. Similarly, the steam-engine technology that would revolutionize the world after 1781 had been under development for decades before then—as already noted, James Watt's first really successful steam engine was completed in 1776, the year of the Declaration of Independence.

Neptune, as its astrological influences would suggest, was less abrupt and unexpected in its appearance, and a span of thirty years preceding its discovery neatly brackets the emergence of the Neptunian current. The revolutions of 1848 and the radical thought given its conclusive form by Marx and Engels were both results of ideologies that had been spreading throughout Europe since shortly after the Napoleonic Wars ended in 1815, promoted by organizations such as the Carbonari and individuals such as Filippo Buonarroti, the pioneering ideologue of the revolution of the masses. Similarly, European fantastic literature saw its first significant stirrings in the writings of German author E. T. A. Hoffmann, whose publications appeared between 1814 and 1825, and Thomas de Quincey's *Confessions of an English Opium-Eater,* the first significant work in the modern literature of drug abuse, first saw print in 1821.

This gradual onset of planetary influence is important to the broader story we're tracing. The thirty-year orbital period of Saturn quite consistently seems to measure the process by which a new planetary influences comes into play. This is not surprising, since Saturn is the astrological ruler of time and a thirty-year interval also measures neatly the time needed for the first members of a new generation to reach an age where they can begin to have a significant effect on their culture. The thirty-year onset period can be traced in another story of astronomical discovery from the same period—the saga of Ceres, the planet that turned out not to be a planet after all. As we'll see, the history of Ceres also marks out the comparable thirty-year period during which the influence of a former planet fades out.

THREE

The Cerean Era

On the night of January 1, 1801, Giuseppe Piazzi was peering into the eyepiece of a telescope in Palermo, Sicily. A Catholic monk whose repeated clashes with the hierarchy of the Church had cost him a string of more prestigious academic jobs, Piazzi had ended up as the director of the Palermo Observatory, tasked with such exciting duties as checking the accuracy of star catalogs, one star at a time. That's what he was doing that night, making sure a minor star in Taurus was where one catalog said it was, when he spotted another dim star close to the one he was observing—a star that was not in the catalog he was checking, or for that matter any other.

The next night, when he turned the telescope to the same part of Taurus, the dim star had moved slightly. The same thing happened on the nights of January 3 and 4. Bad weather made observations impossible for the next few nights, but on the 10th Piazzi found the same dim star again, and it was still moving against the background of stars. He continued watching it until February 11, when an attack of illness made further work impossible. In the meantime, on January 25, he wrote to his friend and fellow astronomer Johann Elert Bode to let him know about the little dot of light moving through Taurus.

The letter didn't come as a complete surprise to Bode, or to his astronomical colleagues. In 1772 the German mathematician Johann Daniel Titius had noted that the solar system's known planets followed a curious mathematical progression in their orbits. If the distance from the Sun to Mercury was arbitrarily set at 4 units, Venus was 4 + 3 units from the Sun, Earth 4 + 6, and Mars 4 + 12. There was no known planet at 4 + 24 units from the Sun, but then Jupiter came at 4 + 48 units and Saturn at 4 + 96.

Piazzi's friend Bode had discussed the same progression in a book he published in 1773. In 1781, when Sir William Herschel discovered Uranus, Bode noted that the new planet was located not quite 4 + 128 units out from the Sun. The Titius-Bode Law, as the progression came to be called, led several astronomers (Bode among them) to hypothesize that another undiscovered planet was lurking in the gap between Mars and Jupiter.

It was another German astronomer, Baron Franz Xavier von Zach, who came up with the idea of a cooperative hunt for the missing planet. After several meetings with others interested in the problem, Zach organized a group—wryly naming it the Celestial Police—to hunt down the fugitive, and wrote letters to astronomers all over Europe, inviting them to join the pursuit. Piazzi was one of the recipients and realized fairly quickly that the little moving light he had spotted might well fit the all-points bulletin the Celestial Police had issued.

Zach immediately announced the discovery, but the fugitive was not quite ready to give up yet. News of the discovery took its time getting to Bode and Zach in Germany (Napoleon had launched his invasion of Italy in the first months of 1801 so there was some excuse for the delay). By the time Zach could circulate the details in his monthly newsletter, Piazzi's dim star was hiding behind the Sun. It was autumn before the search could begin again, and the handful of observations Piazzi had been able to make weren't enough to allow astronomers to calculate the body's orbit using the methods known at the time. Zach and his colleagues tried their best, but for a time it seemed as though the fugitive planet had evaded detection.

Fortunately for the Celestial Police, they had an equivalent of Sherlock Holmes on call. This was Carl Friedrich Gauss, one of the greatest mathematicians of all time, who liked to relax in his off hours by doing the kind of number crunching that gets assigned to high-speed computers nowadays. Gauss took Piazzi's handful of observations and, inventing a completely new method of orbital calculation in the process, predicted where the missing planet would be. On December 7, 1801, following Gauss's guidance, Zach spotted the runaway again.

Bad weather intervened, but the Celestial Police were not about to be thrown off the track a second time. On January 1, 1802, Zach and another member of the Police, Heinrich Olbers, finally cornered the fugitive and spread the word. There was a great deal of discussion about what to name the newly discovered body, but Piazzi's suggestion—Ceres, after the Roman goddess of agriculture and patroness of Piazzi's homeland of Sicily—was ultimately adopted by everybody.

Piazzi, Bode, Zach, and all the other astronomers involved in the discovery were convinced that they had discovered an unknown planet, just as William Herschel had done twenty years before. Other astronomers across Europe agreed with them, and Ceres duly took its place in books on astronomy among the planets, filling the gap between Mars and Jupiter. Then, less than three months after Ceres was finally brought to heel, Heinrich Olbers was studying the new planet through a telescope and found yet another little star near it, where no star was supposed to be. He got over his surprise quickly enough to track the new planet and send the details to Gauss, who promptly worked out the orbit. The new planet, Pallas, turned out to be in the same gap between Mars and Jupiter as Ceres, at nearly the same distance from the Sun.

That was baffling. More baffling still was the first size estimate for the new planets, which was made by William Herschel, the discoverer of Uranus. Though his calculation was off by a significant factor—not surprisingly, since the equipment astronomers had available at the time for making the necessary measurements was still extremely crude—he figured out, correctly, that the new planets were a small fraction of the size of Mercury or the Moon. He argued on that basis that they didn't count as planets at all, and suggested that they be called *asteroids,* from a Greek word meaning "starlike."

Few people listened at first. As it turned out, though, Ceres and Pallas weren't alone in the belt of space where the Titius-Bode Law had predicted another planet. Two others, Juno and Vesta, were discovered in 1804 and 1807 respectively. A fifth, Astraea, turned up in 1845, and fourteen more had been spotted by 1851. By then, though, their status as planets had been challenged more decisively by the discovery of Neptune in 1846. Neptune, with a diameter almost four times Earth's, was a planet by anybody's reckoning. With a diameter less than a thirteenth of Earth's, by contrast, Ceres was another matter, and all of Ceres's sister worldlets were much smaller than she was.

As a result, beginning around 1850, astronomy textbooks and popular works on the subject quietly stopped referring to Ceres and her sisters as planets, and adopted Herschel's term *asteroids* instead. There was no international body tasked with keeping track of celestial objects in those days—the International Astronomical Union was not given that responsibility until 1919—and so, unlike Pluto, Ceres was not voted out of planetary status by a panel of astronomers. Instead, the change happened one textbook and encyclopedia at a time. Chapters on "The Fifth, Sixth, Seventh, and Eighth Planets," which is how Ceres, Pallas, Juno, and Vesta were numbered during their glory days, were quietly replaced with chapters on "The Asteroids," and Jupiter regained his former place as the fifth planet from the Sun.

THE CEREAN ERA IN ASTROLOGY

During the years when Ceres was considered a planet, astrology was still recovering from the near-death experience it had passed through a few centuries earlier, and those astrologers who had the time and inclination for original research seem to have kept themselves busy sorting out the influence of Uranus. If Ceres had stayed a planet longer, doubtless the astrological community would have gotten to her in due time, but that counts as one of history's many might-have-beens.

As we've seen, however, doubts about Ceres's planetary status emerged quite early on, and the discovery of Neptune completed the process of convincing astrologers as well as astronomers that Ceres and her sisters belonged among the small fry of the solar system. I know of no significant research into the astrological properties of any of the asteroids before the twentieth century, and even when that research got under way in that century it was the preoccupation of a small minority of astrologers.

The year 1986 saw this general lack of interest begin to shift, with the publication of Demetra George's groundbreaking book *Asteroid Goddesses*. George had carried out a great deal of original research into the effects of the four asteroids Ceres, Pallas, Juno, and Vesta on the horoscopes she studied, and was able to sketch out the influences of these four bodies in some detail. Other astrologers since that time have added their own efforts to George's research, and as a result the astrological influence of Ceres and her sisters is becoming fairly well recognized at present.

To sum up this influence, Ceres—now, of course, raised out of the asteroids to the status of a dwarf planet—is the astrological body that rules nourishment and nurturing. The place where it appears in your natal chart, and the planets with which it makes aspects in that chart, can show how you relate to food, and more generally your relationship to nurturing and being nurtured. When it is afflicted in your natal chart by difficult aspects, it shows where you will lack nurturing, and therefore it can be associated with loss and depression. The aspects it makes to your natal chart over time by transit and progression can tell you when issues involving food and nurturing, or their absence, will become important to you.

Ceres is unquestionably a minor influence, much less potent and rather narrower in focus than any of the planets. If it is weakly placed in your birth chart and has no important aspects to other planets, you may not feel its effects at all. In charts where it is strongly placed and has significant aspects, however, its influence is significant enough to be worth tracking. As we'll see, this distinction helps to make sense of the astrological meanings of dwarf planets in general, and thus points toward insights that will be important later on in this book.

The astrology of Ceres has another special importance for the theme explored here, because astrologers weren't the only people who began to give Ceres a second look in the last decades of the twentieth century. During the time that it became clear to astronomers that Pluto didn't really belong among the planets, it became just as clear that Ceres didn't really belong among the asteroids. Ceres is much bigger than any other asteroid—so much so that she accounts for a third of the mass of the entire asteroid belt—and she is large enough that, unlike any other asteroid, her gravity has formed her into a sphere, like a planet, a dwarf planet, or one of the larger moons. Unlike the planets, though, Ceres's gravity is not strong enough to clear the region of space through which she orbits.

As a result, the same 2006 meeting of the International Astronomical Union that demoted Pluto from the ranks of the planets promoted Ceres out of the ranks of the asteroids and assigned both these bodies to the newly formed category of dwarf planet. It is worth noting, in the light of our broader theme, that this happened just thirty years after Demetra George's book revived interest in Ceres among the astrological community.

THE CEREAN ERA IN HISTORY

Like the epochs marked by the discoveries of Uranus and Neptune, the Cerean era began well before the actual moment of discovery, and in this case the arrival of the new influence can be dated quite exactly. The first serious inquiries into the possibility of a planet between Mars and Jupiter followed the publication of the Titius-Bode Law in 1772—just thirty years, please note, before the Celestial Police caught their fugitive once and for all. That same year saw the publication of the first version of iconic German poet and author Johann Wolfgang von Goethe's poem *Prometheus,* which was Goethe's first important publication and one of the first landmarks in the history of the Romantic movement in literature and art. Goethe's first novel *The Sorrows of Young Werther,* which saw print in 1774, became the first Romantic bestseller. In that same year, Thomas Jones's painting *The Bard* played an important role in launching Romanticism in the visual arts.

By the time Piazzi saw a little moving light in Taurus in early 1800, in turn, Romanticism had become the most influential artistic movement of the era, shaping the creative visions of literally hundreds of authors, poets, painters, playwrights, and more—there was even a Romantic style of chess playing. Among Romantic figures still famous today are Byron, Coleridge, Keats, Shelley, and Wordsworth in poetry; Charlotte and Emily Brontë, Nathaniel Hawthorne, and Sir Walter Scott in fiction; and Delacroix, Goya, and the painters of the Hudson River School in painting. It remained a potent influence on culture, society, and the arts until around 1850, when it began to drop out of fashion. By 1880 or so, the Romantic Movement was effectively gone.

In terms of the astrology of history, in other words, Romanticism is the keynote of the Cerean era. This is particularly interesting in terms of the broader story we're exploring, because until the discovery of Neptune, the Cerean influence served as the primary cultural and political opposition to Uranus. The Industrial Revolution, the supreme achievement of the Uranian era, was among the things the Romantics opposed most forcefully. They glorified the Middle Ages, sought inspiration from folktales, and considered powerful emotions more important and more true than rational calculation and proof. Romantic literature and art are colorful, passionate, visionary, and typically draw much of their inspiration from nature or from the events of the distant past. Where the Uranian influence stresses the solitary individual moving into an unknown future, the Cerean influence focuses on the community—not the Neptunian masses—rooted in the rich soil of shared history and experiences.

It also had a political dimension—the movement called romantic nationalism. Nationalism of one kind or another goes back into the distant past, where it links up with tribal loyalties that are likely as old as our species. The romantic nationalism that emerged in the last years of the eighteenth century was a distinct phenomenon, however. It drew on an essentially mystical and emotional concept of the nation as a shared unity of consciousness that joined the living and the dead, in which landscape, history, language, and national culture were all tokens of a reality transcending space and time. It was from within this viewpoint, for example, that the Romantic poet Adam Mickiewicz could envision his native Poland as the Christ of the nations, whose sufferings under Russian occupation would one day redeem the world. It was also from within the viewpoint of romantic nationalism that the concept of Manifest Destiny seized the imagination of the young United States and drove its policy of westward expansion straight across the continent to the shores of the Pacific. The time frame is worth noting here, as in the other cases we've surveyed. Romantic nationalism emerged in response to the American and French Revolutions, had its high tide between 1801 and the 1850s, and faded out thereafter.

As with those other planets, furthermore, issues of place are also significant. While the Cerean influence was felt to one degree or another all over the world, some of its most typical impacts landed first and hardest in Italy, the country from which it was discovered. Romantic nationalism played a crucial part in the *Risorgimento,* the struggle for Italian reunification and independence, which began shortly after Napoleon's conquest of Italy in 1799 to 1800 and reached its fulfillment with the establishment of the Kingdom of Italy in 1861. Romanticism in the arts took very deep root in Italy as well—the great difference between Italian and German opera in the nineteenth century, for example, can be summed up neatly by saying that Italian opera is full of Cerean Romanticism while German opera is far more deeply shaped by Neptunian fantasy.

Yet fantasy continued to inspire new creations long after the

Romantic impulse was spent. One of the things that stands out most strikingly about the Romantic movement, in fact, is just how opaque so many of its products became once it was over. *The Sorrows of Young Werther,* the first Romantic bestseller, is a perfect case in point. It's the story of a love triangle gone wrong: the young poet Werther falls in love with his best friend's wife, all three of the characters involved agonize loudly and at great length over the tragedy of his emotions, and then Werther kills himself. When this tale first saw print, in the dawning years of the Cerean era, it became an overnight success and the subject of fascinated and horrified discussions across Europe. Its emotional impact was so great that it spawned a wave of copycat suicides, in which fans of the story killed themselves in imitation of Werther. Nowadays most people find Goethe's story unreadable, and Werther's over-the-top wallowing in his feelings in particular tends to inspire disgust or laughter rather than sympathy. It made a compelling emotional appeal to people while the planetary influence that inspired it was present, but once that influence faded out, so did its capacity to stir its readers' imaginations and hearts.

Just as the arrival of a new planet marks the appearance of a previously unknown set of influences on human life, the downgrading of a former planet to minor-body status marks the fading out of those influences, and the same approximate time frame of thirty years governs both processes. It's a pattern we can see at work in other examples from history. What makes this fascinating is that it is not limited to bodies such as Ceres, which rose to planetary status and then were downgraded as their true scale became clear. The same pattern shaped the strange history of two "planets," which were apparently discovered in the nineteenth century, but then turned out to have never existed at all.

FOUR

Phantoms of Heaven

By 1859 Urbain Le Verrier was arguably the world's most famous astronomer. He had followed up his co-discovery of Neptune with reams of exquisitely precise calculations in other fields of planetary astronomy, and also took an enthusiastic part in the kind of brutal academic infighting that, then as now, is an essential part of a successful scientist's career. Beginning in 1852 he set out to make his reputation permanent by working out the mathematics of the inner solar system so precisely that no one would ever have to do the job again. Mars, Earth, and Venus duly yielded to the same methods that had tracked down Neptune, and Le Verrier's position in the astronomical world became accordingly more secure.

Mercury was a much harder nut to crack. Le Verrier had tried to work out its movements mathematically in the 1840s, only to find that his best calculations didn't quite match the planet's behavior. When he turned his attention back to the innermost planet in the 1850s, equipped with newer and more precise observations from astronomers, it became clear to him that some unexpected influence must be affecting Mercury's movements. Factor out the gravitational influence of the Sun and all the other planets, and something else seemed to be tugging Mercury's orbit back and forth in a predictable fashion. The obvious suspect was an unknown planet somewhere nearby. Since no trace of such a planet had been spotted over the thousands of years that astronomers had been watching the skies, he decided that it must be located inside the orbit of Mercury, and thus too close to the Sun to be spotted easily. In 1859 Le Verrier published an article suggesting that an undiscovered planet, smaller than Mercury, circled the Sun somewhere inside Mercury's orbit.

Having predicted his new planet, Le Verrier—who was a pen-and-paper astronomer rather than an expert with telescopes—then faced the challenge of having someone find it. As noted earlier, Mercury is far and away the hardest of the classical planets to see, because it is so close to the Sun and so appears only briefly now and then just before sunrise or just after sunset, when the sky is light enough that seeing it at all is a challenge. Since the hypothetical planet Le Verrier had predicted was even nearer the Sun, it could be spotted only through extremely careful or lucky observations, using special equipment. By 1859, however, astronomy was potentially up to the task, and Le Verrier thought he had a real chance of becoming the only astronomer in history to discover two planets.

What Le Verrier did not yet know was that an amateur astronomer in central France, Dr. Edmond Lescarbault, had already spotted something that looked like the newly predicted planet. Once Le Verrier's prediction got splashed over the media, Lescarbault contacted the famous astronomer with details of his sighting: a small bright object about a quarter the apparent diameter of Mercury, very close to the Sun. Word spread rapidly among astronomers and then hit the newspapers, and a search back through old records turned up other little bright spots close to the Sun that might have been the same planet. By early 1860 the astronomical community and the general public had by and large accepted that a new planet needed to be added to the list of the solar system's known worlds. Being so close to the Sun, it could only have one possible name: Vulcan, the divine blacksmith who labored at the fiery forge of the gods.

The one difficulty in this saga of discovery was that other astronomers who went looking for Vulcan came up empty-handed. A few claimed to spot it from time to time, but never quite where Le Verrier's predictions claimed it would be. During the solar eclipse of 1878, which offered near-perfect viewing conditions for the elusive planet, one astronomer claimed to have spotted it, but half a dozen others of equal reputation saw nothing. Gradually support for the supposed planet trickled away. All that remained was the annoying discrepancy in Mercury's motion, and that went away forever on a November day in 1915, when a young physicist named Albert Einstein presented a paper to the Prussian Academy of Sciences in Berlin.

Einstein in 1915 was in the midst of the most dazzling period of his career. He had just completed working out his theory of General Relativity, with its dizzying redefinitions of space and time. Among the consequences of that theory were certain small but important changes in the mathematics of gravity, the first significant revisions in the understanding of gravity since Isaac Newton's time. The unexplained wobble in Mercury's orbit offered a perfect opportunity to check Einstein's theory, and the paper he presented in Berlin that day showed that his new understanding of gravity accounted perfectly for the oddities of Mercury's motion. By the time he finished reading his paper, as far as scientific astronomy was concerned, the phantom planet Vulcan had disappeared forever.

Meanwhile, as Vulcan passed through the arc of its strange history, another apparent saga of planetary discovery was under way a good deal closer to home. In 1846 Frédéric Petit, director of the Toulouse Observatory, announced that certain slight wobbles in the Moon's motions were best explained by the presence of a much smaller second moon in a highly elliptical orbit, closer to the Earth than the Moon—so close, in fact, that it would have had to pass through Earth's atmosphere. Three astronomers, two at Toulouse and one at Artenac, promptly caught sight of something that looked like a small second moon. Though pioneer science fiction writer Jules Verne borrowed Petit's moon as a plot point in his 1865 space travel thriller *Around the Moon,* most astronomers rejected the theory, and other attempts to chase down the second moon with telescopes turned up nothing.

There the story of Earth's second moon languished until 1898, when the German astronomer Georg Waltemath published a paper claiming to prove the existence of a second natural satellite of the Earth. Unlike Petit's moon, Waltemath's was located out well beyond the Moon, and took 119 days to orbit the Earth. He also claimed that it was made of an extremely dark substance, and thus reflected so little light that it was normally invisible. Twelve people nonetheless claimed to have sighted it during one of its brief periods of visibility, shortly after the publication of Waltemath's paper, and Waltemath also found earlier sightings of faint objects described in the astronomical literature, which appeared to confirm his moon's existence.

Waltemath's moon found an eccentric defender in 1907, when the Canadian writer Ezekiel Stone Wiggins announced that the second moon was responsible for that year's unusually cold winter. Wiggins was one of those astonishing figures that pop up from time to time to confound those people who like to think of Canada as the dull northern neighbor of the United States. A pioneering cryptozoologist who believed that plesiosaurs still swam the Atlantic, the author of an early science fiction novel and an assortment of argumentative books on theology and cosmology, and an unsuccessful candidate for Canada's Parliament, Wiggins claimed to be able to predict storms, earthquakes, and epidemics by means of complicated formulas of his own invention (the fact that he scored far more misses than hits never succeeded in denting his immense self-confidence).

His efforts on behalf of Waltemath's moon did nothing for its scientific reputation but helped bring it to the attention of astrologer Walter Gorn Old, who gave the moon its enduring name: Lilith, after the legendary first wife of Adam. A few other observers claimed from time to time to spot something that might have been the dark moon Lilith, but nearly all astronomers dismissed these claims, and most attempts to observe it yielded no results at all. Like Vulcan, it promptly vanished from the heavens as astronomers knew them.

VULCAN AND LILITH IN ASTROLOGY

Vulcan achieved a few years of acceptance by the astronomical community before fading out into the realm of might-have-beens, while the phantom moons of Petit and Waltemath never found acceptance at all. Both these strays of the heavens, however, were promptly adopted by some astrologers, who did the same thing that their peers were doing with Uranus and Neptune—casting charts with the placements of the new planets included and seeing how they interacted with the known planets against the background of the signs and houses.

In both cases, the adoption papers were signed by an influential figure of the occult scene of the time. In Vulcan's case the figure in question was the redoubtable Helena Petrovna Blavatsky: mystic, bestselling author, and cofounder of the Theosophical Society, the most influential organization in the late nineteenth-century revival of Western esoteric spirituality. Blavatsky liked to entertain her followers and annoy her opponents by pointing out places where the scientific and religious orthodoxies of her time failed to match up to everyday experience, and she occasionally extended the same favor to her rivals in the alternative spirituality scene. Vulcan made a convenient theme for such sallies—why didn't modern astrologers know about it, since the secretive Mahatmas to whom she credited her teachings surely did?

That was more than enough encouragement to give other authors of alternative thinking, then and afterward, an excuse to put Vulcan into their cosmologies. Alice Bailey, Max Heindel, and George Winslow Plummer were among the leading occult writers of the early twentieth century, and all of them found a place for Vulcan in their accounts of the cosmos. Some astrologers, especially those who drew heavily on occult traditions, promptly followed suit. Books and pamphlets tracking Vulcan through the signs duly appeared. Some of those are still in print, and most full-featured horoscope programs available today include Vulcan as an optional planet. The great majority of astrologers, however, never included Vulcan in their charts, and it remains a specialty interest in today's astrological community.

A stranger version of the same fate awaited the dark moon Lilith, once her existence had been proclaimed by Waltemath. The idea of a dark satellite of Earth had been in circulation in the occult community, curiously enough, well before Waltemath's time. The Hermetic Brotherhood of Luxor, one of the most influential occult organizations of the 1880s, included the existence of that spectral body in its teachings, and when Thomas Burgoyne's *The Light of Egypt* made those teachings publicly available in 1889, the presence of a dark moon orbiting the Earth became a common theme of occult speculation.

The dark satellite described by Burgoyne was thoroughly evil, the kingdom of the "dark hierarch Ob" and the focal point of all the negative moral energies that afflict human beings on Earth. Like Petit's moon, Burgoyne's dark satellite also found its way into the imaginative fiction of the era, where it kept the same evil character it had been assigned by occultists. To cite one example out of several, *The Slayer of Souls,* a rousing if somewhat formulaic 1920 occult adventure novel by popular novelist Robert W. Chambers (much better known today as the author of *The King in Yellow*), had a mysterious dark satellite of Earth radiating evil magic as an important piece of its plot machinery.

The English astrologer Walter Gorn Old, who wrote under the pen name Sepharial, may well have been influenced by Burgoyne. Certainly, he began studying Waltemath's moon and tracking its location in horoscopes as soon as press reports of its discovery reached him. In his 1918 book, *The Science of Foreknowledge,* he included several chapters on the astrology of Lilith, including a number of case studies. He described Lilith's influence in terms very similar to Burgoyne's, as "undoubtedly obstructive and fatal, productive of various forms of catastrophes and accidents, sudden upsets, changes, and states of confusion."

Later astrologers put their own interpretation on the dark moon, identifying it as the planet of temptation and self-undoing, of seduction and sexual charisma, of feminine sexuality, and of women's liberation, according to the gender politics of the astrologer. In her 1961 book, *The Black Moon Lilith,* for example, Ivy Goldstein-Jacobson described Lilith in Burgoynesque terms as "sinister and malevolent, denying, frustrating, and catastrophic." In her 1988 article, "Lilith—the Dark Moon," by contrast, Carr Foy paints a very different picture: "Lilith lives behind-the-scenes, usually undetected. She can be sneaky or deceptive, but she can also indicate our ability to be subtle, to guide and manage events and people without being intrusive. She is our ability to be private, and her placement in the chart will tell you what the native feels most secretive about. As a Moon, Lilith is also associated with mothering, but she is the strength of a mother protecting her cubs."

Even more transformations were to come. Over the course of the twentieth century, a group of French astrologers reassigned the name Lilith to a different point in the heavens, defined by the orbit of the Moon. Like all orbits in space, that of the Moon is an ellipse rather than a circle, and geometrically speaking, every ellipse has two foci rather than a single center; the Earth occupies one focus of the Moon's elliptical orbit, but the other is empty. That empty focus, according to the French school, is the black (rather than "dark") moon Lilith.

Due to the complexities of the Moon's motion, there's a difference between the true position of the empty focus and its mean or average position; some of the handful of astrologers who work with the black moon Lilith use one, while some use the other. Finally, a small asteroid discovered in 1927 is named Lilith, and some astrologers use this body as a marker for the Lilith influence. So, there are four Liliths in the astrological heavens, and among those astrologers who use any of them—a very small minority in today's astrological community, be it noted—there is no consensus as to which of these points should be used.

VULCAN AND LILITH IN HISTORY

The strange careers of Vulcan and Lilith make excellent test cases for the core thesis of this book—the proposal that the discovery of a new planet and the disappearance or demotion of an existing body are not simply products of variations in the opinions of astronomers, but that they reflect significant changes in the constellations of astrological forces that define the inner landscape of human life. If this is true, the apparent "discovery" of a nonexistent planet should mark the rise of a cluster of influences that are related to the planet's symbolism—a set of influences, which were expected to emerge as a major independent factor in human life, but never quite got around to doing so. In this case, the final disproof of the imaginary planet would mark the failure of that expectation and the absorption of the influences in existing patterns of consciousness and astrological influence: in each case, with something close to the usual thirty-year period of emergence and fading out before and after.

In the case of Vulcan, exactly this pattern stands out insistently from the historical data. Vulcan was "discovered" in 1860 and disproved in 1915, and the hypothetical Vulcanian era thus began in 1830 and ended in 1945. Vulcan in mythology is the blacksmith and technologist of the gods, the inventor of metal objects that moved by themselves. It is thus surely no accident that the period from 1830 to 1945, while Vulcan's influence was in process, was the greatest era of technological innovation in human history, the period during which most of the technologies that define modern life were first invented and put to work. The steamship, the railroad, the dynamo, the telephone, the light bulb, the radio, the automobile, the submarine, the airplane, the television, the jet engine, the guided missile, the computer, and more—all these were part of the vast and unparalleled outpouring of technological wizardry that took place during the Vulcanian era, typified by charismatic inventors such as Thomas Edison and Nikola Tesla.

Yet technology in the Vulcanian era was surrounded by a halo of social expectations that turned out to be wildly inaccurate. These can best be seen in the two great science fiction authors of the Vulcanian era, Jules Verne and H. G. Wells, whose novels served as lightning rods for the collective imagination of humanity during that time. For both these authors and their many imitators, technological innovation was a wild card that inevitably challenged existing social and political structures. In Verne's novels, especially, each of the technological leaps he foresaw was the creation of an individual genius at odds with the establishment of his time, and very often resulted in the inventor going to war with society, either striking from the fringes (Captain Nemo in *Twenty Thousand Leagues under the Sea*) or using an immense technological edge to conquer the world (Robur in *Robur the Conqueror*).

That was not the way things played out, however. Instead of becoming an independent influence on society, technological innovation was taken over and redirected by existing centers of political and economic power. The point at which this process was complete can be tracked easily enough by watching the widening mismatch between popular ideas and the realities of technological development. In the very few works of fiction about nuclear weapons written before the Second World War—for example, Eric Ambler's 1936 spy thriller *The Dark Frontier*—it was assumed as a matter of course that those weapons would be created by an individual, eccentric scientific genius for purposes of his own. Equally, novels about space travel written at the same time—for example, C. S. Lewis's 1938 science fiction novel *Out of the Silent Planet*—assumed just as universally that the first spacecraft would be produced, tested, and launched by individual inventors in the privacy of their own laboratories, in much the same way that the first powered airplane was created by the Wright brothers.

As it turned out, of course, neither of those expectations turned out to be correct. Instead, vast governmental programs funded by taxpayers, directed by sprawling bureaucracies, and subservient to the established order of society, were needed to create the atomic bomb, launch rockets into space, and so on. The detonation of the first atomic bomb can serve as the marker for that shift, and that event took place in 1945—the year that the Vulcanian influence in human history reached its end.

Even though it did not actually exist, in other words, Vulcan functioned as an astrological planet for a period of 115 years. Grant the basic presuppositions of astrology and Vulcan's apparent discovery and final disproof were just as precisely shaped by the heavens as all other events here on Earth. Its keynote as an astrological planet can be identified as *technology as an independent force in human affairs*. In simpler and more colorful terms, Vulcan was the planet of that pervasive icon of pop culture—the mad scientist. The beginning of its influence marks the point at which such a figure became conceivable, the period when it functioned as a planet frames the years when such figures very nearly came into existence, and the end of its influence marks the point at which cutting-edge scientific research stopped being an activity of eccentric individuals and turned into the exclusive prerogative of big government and big business.

As its varied symbolism would suggest, the dark moon Lilith is a far more elusive influence than Vulcan, and the beginning and ending of the era in which she was an active force in human affairs is harder to trace due to the vagaries of its history. If the dark moon is identified solely with Waltemath's moon, its influence would extend from 1868 to 1928—thirty years to each side of the date of its supposed discovery. If the dark moon is identified with Petit's moon on the one hand, and with the cluster of competing Lilith-points in current astrology on the other, the Lilithian era began in 1816 and hasn't ended yet. Here again a close look at history with an eye sharpened by the mythic symbolism of Lilith reveals a pattern impossible to ignore.

In Jewish mythology Lilith was the first wife of Adam, who refused to accept a subordinate position to him and was therefore transformed into a nocturnal child-eating demon. In her image we can see the shadow-side of the feminine brought into vivid focus—and exactly that theme, the theme of woman as demon and devourer, seized the collective imagination of much of the world during the late Victorian period and remained in place until the era between the two world wars. In his thorough study of the theme, *Idols of Perversity*, art historian and cultural critic Bram Dijkstra has shown how Victorian culture became obsessed with a stark terror of human (and especially female) sexuality and defended itself against that terror by an immense structure of pretense that denied that women had any sexual desires at all.

The resulting fixation on the sexless, selfless "angel in the house" inevitably called up its opposite, the alluring, devouring woman-demon who haunted the arts and the collective imagination of the late nineteenth and early twentieth centuries. In astrological terms, the Victorian era tried to pretend that the Moon had no dark side, and that dark side promptly constellated into an independent astrological force in its own right. It also crystallized into a new social reality, for the era of Lilith also turned out to be the season of the witch.

The reinvention of witchcraft as a modern feminist religion has already begun to attract its historians, but it is the prehistory of the movement that deserves our attention here. The idea that the witches of the Middle Ages had belonged to an organized pagan religion surviving from ancient times seems to have been invented by French historian Jules Michelet in his 1862 book, *Satanism and Witchcraft,* a little more than thirty years before Waltemath's moon had its brief day. The identification of that hypothetical cult with feminist themes was the work of pioneering feminist Matilda Joslyn Gage, whose 1893 book *Woman, Church and State* argued that the witches of the Middle Ages had been pagan priestesses of a goddess-centered religion dating from ancient times, nine million of whom were burnt at the stake by the Christian church. That in turn inspired Charles Godfrey Leland, who in 1899—the year after Waltemath's apparent discovery of a second moon—published *Aradia, or the Gospel of the Witches.* Leland claimed that the text at the heart of his book was a surviving scripture of Michelet's and Gage's witch-cult that Leland had obtained from an Italian witch. As with nearly everything associated with Lilith, that claim remains contested to this day.

In the first half of the twentieth century, Margaret Murray and Robert Graves picked up the supposed pagan witchcraft of Gage and Leland and took the process to the next stage. Murray, an Egyptologist with no training in medieval European history, wrote three books claiming to prove the existence of the medieval witch-cult. Her books were widely accepted until later scholars demonstrated that she had deliberately twisted her sources over and over again to make them fit her theory. Graves, a poet and novelist, penned a very strange book titled *The White Goddess,* "a historical grammar of poetic myth," that presented the worship of a Lilith-esque moon goddess as the original true faith of humanity, overlaid by patriarchal god-cults. Finally, over the course of the 1940s, Murray's close friend Gerald Gardner finished the process of bringing Lilith's influence down to Earth with the creation of his newly minted "old religion" of Wicca, the first and most typical of the modern neopagan religions, and the inspiration for a galaxy of witchcraft groups all over the industrial world.

Over the course of its emergence, however, modern feminist witchcraft veered away from the Lilith image in crucial ways and shed all but the thinnest veneer of opposition to the status quo of contemporary society. Over the course of the century following the publication of Gage's book, after all, the attitudes toward sexuality and gender politics that she promoted had become the conventional wisdom, not only in the affluent liberal circles where modern feminist witchcraft found its largest audience, but also in the media, the universities, and the mainstream of public discourse in most Western countries.

Modern feminist witchcraft thus joined up with many other would-be transgressive movements of the same period and spent its time going through the motions of rebelling against the world of its adherents' grandparents while giving wholehearted support to the supposedly progressive establishment of its own time. At the same time, the alluring and frightening witch of fin-de-siècle culture gave way to the wholesome, fresh-faced Wiccan of today's popular culture, with "An it harm none!" forever on her lips. When historian Ronald Hutton titled his survey of the origins of Wicca *The Triumph of the Moon,* he was, among other things, providing a neat summary of an astrological fact. While the imaginary dark moon Lilith presided over the prehistory of modern feminist witchcraft, the familiar Moon took over its birth and history, leaving Lilith to fade into the realm of might-have-beens.

FIVE

The Plutonian Era

The astronomical, astrological, and cultural themes we've traced up to this point all bear directly on the central theme of this book, because the rise and fall of Pluto as an astrological planet and a reality in human collective consciousness can't be understood at all if its history is taken out of context. By the time Pluto was first sighted in 1930, it bears remembering, astronomers and astrologers alike had plenty of experience in dealing with newly discovered planets. By the time Pluto was demoted to minor planet status in 2006, equally, both astronomers and astrologers had been through that process of demotion more than once as well. These previous experiences make it easier to see through the sometimes-overheated passions that surround the Plutonian era and gauge what that era has meant—and what its ending will mean.

As with those previous examples, we can begin with the history of Pluto's discovery. The quest for Pluto goes back further than many people realize, for the possibility that there might be another undiscovered planet out beyond Neptune had been discussed even before Neptune was discovered in the first place. Already in 1834, when the vagaries of the orbit of Uranus were a hot topic in scientific discussions, the German astronomer Peter Hansen suggested that two planets beyond Uranus might explain the facts better than one. Once Neptune was found in 1846, suggestions along the same lines as Hansen's became commonplace in astronomical literature and stayed there all through the second half of the nineteenth century.

There was good reason for this. When astronomers took the best available data on the orbits of Uranus and Neptune, and tried to make sense of them mathematically, the numbers simply didn't work. Neptune's orbit appeared to have wobbles in it that betrayed the presence of another planet. For that matter, so did Uranus. A comprehensive study of the orbit of Uranus, published in 1900 by Danish astronomer Hans Lau, showed up discrepancies that the gravitational attraction of Neptune didn't appear to explain.

That year saw the beginnings of the first systematic search for the unknown planet by professional astronomers, which turned up nothing but whetted the appetite of the astronomical community for planet-hunting. Percival Lowell, a wealthy Bostonian with a passion for astronomy, joined the hunt in 1904, directing the staff of the observatory he'd founded in Flagstaff, Arizona, to focus their efforts on the trans-Neptunian body that Lowell called "Planet X." There's definite poetic justice in the fact that it was at the Lowell Observatory that a newly hired astronomer named Clyde Tombaugh finally spotted Pluto in 1930.

For a change, the newly discovered planet wasn't named by its discoverer, or by a consensus of experts. Instead, America being America, it was named by public opinion. As Tombaugh and his colleagues tried to come up with a suitable name for the planet, thousands of suggestions poured in. The one that was accepted, Pluto, was coined by an eleven-year-old English schoolgirl named Venetia Burney. It was enthusiastically adopted by the staff of the Lowell Observatory, partly because the dark outer reaches of the solar system made them think of the gloomy underworld where the Greek god Pluto ruled, and partly because the first two letters of the name were also Percival Lowell's initials.

Thus named, the newly discovered planet quickly became a pop culture icon, especially in America, the nation from which it was discovered. Astronomer and science promoter Neil deGrasse Tyson didn't overstate the case when he described Pluto as "America's favorite planet." Walt Disney's 1931 decision to name Mickey Mouse's pet dog Pluto the Pup may have clinched the deal. It's only fair to note, though, that Pluto Water was also the name of one of the era's most popular laxatives, sold under the slogan "When Nature Won't, Pluto Will"—an oddly appropriate omen, given the influences that astrologers would soon trace back to the newly discovered planet.

Before long, Pluto was enshrined as the ninth planet in school textbooks and pop culture alike. Tom Corbett, Space Cadet, went there in the course of his adventures, and pulp-fantasy writer H. P. Lovecraft wove Pluto into his tales of extraterrestrial horror, renaming it "Yuggoth" and stocking it with superhumanly intelligent and highly malevolent fungi. Those of my readers who grew up, as I did, in the middle decades of the twentieth century may recall the gorgeously painted spacescapes by Chesley Bonestell and other illustrators of the same period. Pluto routinely featured in such paintings, a dim, frozen, and oddly romantic world, lit by a tiny pinpoint of a Sun and covered in an eternal blanket of ice.

THE PLUTONIAN ERA IN ASTROLOGY

The discovery of Pluto did not catch astrologers napping. By 1930 astrology had made a complete recovery from its eighteenth-century near-death experience. In place of the scattered handful of astrologers who kept the tradition alive into the early nineteenth century, the astrological community in 1930 was a sizable subculture with its own well-funded schools, journals, publishers, and professional organizations. They were ready to make sense of the new planet as soon as it put in an appearance. A few astrologers in the decades just before 1930 had even noticed the presence of some unfamiliar influence in the zodiacal sign of Cancer, in the vicinity of the malefic fixed star Wasat (delta Geminorum). In the absence of any known planet in that part of the sky, those influences were assigned to Wasat—an interpretation that was changed in a hurry when Clyde Tombaugh spotted Pluto a short distance from that very star.

The initial reaction of astrologers to Pluto's discovery was nonetheless just as cautious as the comparable reactions to Neptune. Llewellyn George, arguably the most influential astrological teacher in the United States when the new planet was announced, was typical: "At the present time," he wrote in post-1930 editions of his classic *A to Z Horoscope Maker and Delineator*, "very little is yet known of Pluto's influence on human affairs." The same methods used earlier to work out the astrological influences of Uranus and Neptune were promptly brought to bear on the newly discovered planet, however, and the vastly larger number of astrologers available to work on the project by the mid-twentieth century made it a much less drawn-out affair than the interpretation of the two earlier planets had been.

It became clear early on that unlike Uranus and Neptune, Pluto had a name that was very much in keeping with its character. Pluto in mythology was the lord of the underworld, and the newly discovered planet had an influence that corresponded closely with that theme, ruling the unconscious mind and the most deeply rooted passions, linking up with the subterranean realities of human existence. Its influences were subversive and seductive, and its effects in natal charts were explosive, transgressive, and transformative, sometimes leading to healing and regeneration, sometimes leading to disintegration and disaster. It showed close connections with death, but also with sexuality and with modes of transformation that amounted to rebirth. Where Uranus brings change from some unexpected quarter, Pluto brought change that erupted from within; where Neptune's effects are subtle, Pluto's were dramatic.

Over the half century following Pluto's discovery, these themes became more and more clearly worked out by astrologers. It became a normal part of astrological practice to check Pluto's position in a birth chart for indications of where unconscious drives were most likely to surface, where unrecognized conflicts were to be found, and to watch for transits of other planets that affected Pluto's natal position and indicated that this or that aspect of a client's life was about to blow sky high as a result of unacknowledged inner conflicts, rooted as often as not in issues relating to sex and death. Since psychoanalysis was in vogue in the Plutonian era, that influence was sometimes overstated by enthusiastic astrologers. Those of my readers who had their birth charts delineated may have had the experience, as I did, of being warned of a massive psychological crisis that turned out to be considerably less trouble than predicted. As we'll see, this habit of overhyping the influence of Pluto wasn't accidental, and it turned out to be a significant theme once Pluto's influence entered its twilight years.

At least one leading astrologer during Pluto's heyday had a more subtle reading of the new planet. In her 1973 book, *Pluto or Minerva: The Choice Is Yours,* American astrologer Isabel M. Hickey predicted on the basis of close analyses of natal charts that a very large moon, nearly large enough to count as a planet, would turn out to be orbiting Pluto. She was of course quite correct; Pluto's chief moon Charon, which was discovered five years after Hickey's book saw print, is nearly half Pluto's size and would count as a dwarf planet in its own right if it didn't orbit Pluto. She named the moon Minerva, after the goddess of wisdom, and proposed that it was possible for individuals to decide which of these planetary energies they would bring into their lives—the disruptive underworld energy of Pluto or the regenerative wisdom of Minerva. Hers remained a minority view, however.

There was good reason for that. During Pluto's heyday, astrologers who treated Pluto as an underworld influence that released hidden tensions in explosive outbursts found that their personality analyses were more accurate and their predictions more exact than those who ignored the new planet or gave it some other significance. As discussed in the introduction to this book, it's impossible to make sense of the Plutonian era without grasping that Pluto was a planet in every astrological sense from the time of its discovery to the time of its demotion, that it had at least some planetary force over a period beginning some thirty years before its discovery, and that it will continue to have at least some planetary force for some thirty years after 2006. What makes the end of the Plutonian era so significant a factor in today's world is not that Pluto was never important—it is that a potent influence that has shaped all our lives is slowly fading out, and we will therefore have to recalibrate our understandings of ourselves and our visions of our destiny in response to the changes that result from that fading.

THE PLUTONIAN ERA IN HISTORY

As we've seen, the eras defined by planetary discoveries quite often begin around the time that the serious search for the planet does, and the Plutonian era was no exception. Equally, the eras defined by planetary discoveries have fairly often begun with a bang, and here, Pluto was an even more dramatic example than usual.

Though the possibility of more than one planet farther out than Uranus was first bruited about well back in the nineteenth century, serious efforts to find Planet X began in 1900, with the publication of Hans Lau's study of Uranus's orbit and the first systematic astronomical search for a world beyond Neptune. That same year saw the publication of Sigmund Freud's *The Interpretation of Dreams,* the first programmatic statement of what would become Freudian psychology. In the following year, 1901, Albert Einstein's first scientific paper was published. Both these new beginnings were promptly followed by a flurry of further publications that shattered some of the Western world's most cherished and unquestioned beliefs about the nature of humanity and the universe.

The parallels between Freud's project and Einstein's are far from superficial. Both men took something that had long been understood as an unbreakable unit—in Freud's case, the individual personality; in Einstein's, the atom—and showed how it could be split (the English words *individual* and *atom*, in fact, come from Greek and Latin terms respectively meaning exactly the same thing: "that which cannot be divided"). As Freud's theory divided the *individuum* into id, ego, and superego, releasing the explosive energy of the libido, so Einstein's theory showed how the *atomos* could be turned into *tomos*, "the divided," splitting the atom and releasing the explosive energy of nuclear power.

These were far from the only Plutonian factors to explode into public awareness in the thirty years prior to Pluto's discovery. In retrospect it's remarkable how many of the social phenomena we've already tracked shifted into a Plutonian mode once the new influence began to be felt. Feminism, to cite only one example out of many, lost its Neptunian quality in the years following 1900—it was in 1903, for example, that Emmeline Pankhurst founded the Women's Social and Political Union, the first suffragist organization to condone violence in the struggle to win the vote for women, and in 1906 that Emma Goldman founded the anarchist-feminist journal *Mother Earth,* which played a crucial role in helping to establish feminism's politically and socially radical wing.

Pankhurst and Goldman were responsible for only relatively minor acts of violence. Some of the other manifestations of Pluto's influence were on the other end of a spectrum traced in human blood. From an astrological standpoint it is anything but accidental that the Second World War, the deadliest war in recorded human history, took place in Pluto's heyday, or that the worst mass murders in human history—the gargantuan genocides in Communist China, the Soviet Union, Nazi Germany, and Khmer Rouge Cambodia—all took place in the years between Pluto's discovery and its demotion. Nor did the sexual revolution of the twentieth century, and the resulting transformation of popular entertainment during that century into a vast carnival of sex and death, come as any surprise to those who were paying attention to planetary influences. As the planet of sex and death, of explosive subterranean impulses bursting free of all restraint, Pluto presided over all these transformations.

This same theme—the shattering of unity by deep and previously unacknowledged forces, yielding a blast of disruptive power—ran all through the history of the world during the first phase of the Plutonian era, the time between the first serious inquiry after the new planet in 1900 and its actual discovery in 1930, and continued to gain strength well into the first decades after Pluto's discovery. We can track that theme through some of its most visible manifestations in the history, technology, and popular culture of the time.

Nuclear Fission

The most self-evidently Plutonian of all of Pluto's expressions in modern times, nuclear fission emerged as a possibility during the dawning of the Plutonian era and became a reality within a decade of Pluto's discovery. Radioactivity itself was discovered in 1898, just before the search for Pluto began. As physicists researched the new phenomenon they had to confront the previously unheard-of possibility that the chemical elements were not as stable as scientists had believed, and that immense and unsuspected forces could be released by their disintegration. As research proceeded, the scientific community had to deal with one transgression of accepted principles after another—elements changing into other elements, new elements never before seen being created by scientific means, even the very fabric of space and time stretching and twisting as though in a funhouse mirror.

Einstein's famous equation $E=mc^2$, first published in 1901, alerted researchers to the immense power that could be liberated by converting mass into energy. From then until 1938, when a team of German scientists in Berlin first succeeded in splitting atoms of uranium, the pace of research and discovery was steady. Once it was clear that nuclear fission was possible, major research projects got promptly under way in Britain, Germany, and the United States, and less lavishly funded programs sprang up in many other countries as well. As these programs proceeded, it became clear that two elements were best suited for making an atomic bomb, and as it happened, both had astrologically appropriate names. Uranium, which occurs in nature, was named after Uranus, the planet of revolutionary change and technological innovation, while plutonium, which does not occur in nature and so has to be made artificially—"When Nature Won't, Pluto Will"—was of course named after the newly discovered planet Pluto.

The coming of the Second World War accelerated the search, since all sides in that conflict realized that whichever major power was able to build an atomic weapon first would have an overwhelming advantage over its enemies. As we all know, the United States won that race decisively, building the first successful nuclear reactor in 1942, testing the first atomic bomb in 1945, and leveling the cities of Hiroshima and Nagasaki with nuclear fireballs shortly thereafter, to force Japan to surrender and announce the arrival of a hoped-for *Pax Americana.*

This steady drumbeat of discovery was paralleled by the ascent of nuclear fission as a theme in popular culture. As soon as physicists began to explore the possibility of splitting the atom, the idea of nuclear fission began to find its way into science fiction. From there it spread into other fictional genres as well—Eric Ambler's 1936 spy thriller *The Dark Frontier,* which centered on the invention of an atomic explosive, is a notable example already cited. More broadly, the theme of a new and secret explosive of unparalleled power percolated through the crawlspaces of pulp fiction in the decades before Hiroshima—Talbot Mundy's lively 1930 adventure novel *Jimgrim,* in which a small band of intrepid heroes has to stop a sinister Asian mastermind wielding such an explosive, is one example out of many. When news media brought word of the Hiroshima bombing to an appalled world in 1945, in other words, many people had already encountered similar ideas in fiction, and the extraordinary popular reaction to the new weapons was shaped in profound ways by those fictional precursors.

Discussions of nuclear power from before the first stirrings of the Plutonian era, by contrast, almost always focused on what later became known as nuclear fusion, not fission. A typical example is Jules Verne's 1870 novel *Twenty Thousand Leagues under the Sea,* in which the submarine *Nautilus* was powered by the same power that drives the Sun. The real-life *Nautilus,* the atomic submarine commissioned by the U.S. Navy in 1954, had to get by on fission power instead of fusion.

The Plutonian era, with its focus on the shattering of unities, was not kind to the dreams of those who wanted to generate power from the union of atoms: only as a destructive force, the mechanism behind the most powerful explosives ever created by human beings, did fusion find a place while Pluto was a planet.

Space Travel

Another important expression of the Plutonian influence was the emergence of the dream, and then the reality, of space travel. The notion of traveling from the Earth to other worlds in the solar system and beyond had been a staple of imaginative fiction since Roman times—the most popular tale penned by Roman comic author Lucian of Samosata, wryly titled *A True Story,* included a voyage to the Moon among the preposterous adventures of its protagonists. The transformation of that concept from a leap of the imagination to a problem for engineers, however, began promptly as the first stirrings of the Plutonian era got under way. The first realistic discussion of spaceflight technology, Konstantin Tsiolkovsky's treatise *The Exploration of Cosmic Space by Means of Reaction Devices,* was published in 1903. Robert Goddard's 1919 paper "A Method of Reaching Extreme Altitudes" introduced the liquid-fueled rocket engine that became the key to successful space travel. Once Pluto was discovered theory promptly became practice. The first rocket to reach space was a German V-2 missile on a test flight in 1944, the first satellite was Russia's *Sputnik I* in 1957, and the first manned spacecraft, Russia's *Vostok I,* made one Earth orbit piloted by cosmonaut Yuri Gagarin in 1961 (it was doubtless inevitable, given the intensely sexual focus of the Plutonian influence, that the rockets that made these and later feats possible all looked remarkably like gigantic metal penises).

As these milestones were met and passed, popular culture responded in an extraordinary fashion. Science fiction, as we have seen, was a product of the Uranian era and an important bearer of Uranian influences, and one of its most striking features before the dawn of the Plutonian influence was thus the astonishing diversity of future technologies it imagined. Consider the works of Jules Verne, the premier science fiction author of the nineteenth century. Of the fifty-four novels in his *Marvelous Voyages* series, which includes all his science fiction, only three deal with space travel in any form. H. G. Wells, whose science fiction novels predicted so many future technologies, wrote a total of fifty-three novels; of those, only two dealt with space travel and one more, the eminently forgettable *Star-Begotten,* dealt with interplanetary relations of a non-technological kind.

That breadth of focus changed decisively as the Plutonian era arrived. By the time Pluto was discovered, science fiction was almost by definition about spaceships and extraterrestrial adventure. Not many years thereafter, most science fiction authors put their stories in what we may as well call the science fiction monofuture, a vast and single-tracked shared narrative of the future in which humanity's expansion into space, first to colonize the other planets of the solar system and then to go soaring out among the stars, was seen as the inevitable next step in humanity's history. Science fiction authors such as Isaac Asimov and Arthur C. Clarke penned works insisting that the monofuture they had envisioned in their stories would surely take place in the decades ahead, and these were marketed—and taken seriously—as nonfiction.

Fantasy fiction, science fiction's Neptunian twin, underwent a transformation of its own that was equally Plutonian but otherwise precisely opposed to the transformation of science fiction. Here the relevant figure was that force of nature, J. R. R. Tolkien, whose gargantuan trilogy *The Lord of the Rings* redefined the entire genre in a new form. Fantasy stories before Tolkien took place as often as not in the world we know, and when they strayed from familiar settings, they had many potential destinations from the prehistoric past through the far future to realms unlike anything in human experience.

In Tolkien's wake fantasy narrowed its focus just as science fiction did, fixating on settings that were straightforward pastiches of early medieval Europe and abandoning the wider realms where earlier fantasists had roamed at will. Where science fiction became obsessed with a monofuture of rocketry and distant planets, fantasy became just as obsessed with an equally monolithic past of swords and sorcery. Even the Plutonian symbolism of sex appeared on cue in fantasy fiction—Tolkien's trilogy was far from the only twentieth-century fantasy, after all, in which gargantuan phallic towers were an inescapable part of the imagined landscape.

Yet fantasy fiction played second fiddle at best all through the years of the Plutonian ascendancy. Science fiction took the lead. Even more than nuclear fission and psychoanalysis, space travel became an anchor for utopian dreams, the central mythology of a secular religion of progress that framed all of human existence as a triumphant march from the caves to the stars. This is not surprising, as the idea of space travel involves the most extreme gap ever opened by a Plutonian phenomenon: the vast emptiness of outer space separating space travelers from the Earth. When Neil Armstrong stepped onto the surface of the Moon in 1969, that separation was complete—at least in the minds of believers in space travel.

Communism

As we saw in chapter 2, the theory of political economy launched on its way by Karl Marx and Friedrich Engels by way of 1848's *Communist Manifesto* and detailed thereafter in the pages of Marx's *Das Kapital*, was a thoroughly Neptunian creation. While Neptune remained the outermost planet in the solar system, Marxism was simply one of many popular theories of radical political and economic reform that found takers mostly on the intellectual and cultural fringes of Western society. Among the things that consigned all these systems of thought to irrelevance was the insistence on the part of their creators that they were the inevitable next stage of human evolution. Marx's claim that the revolution whose arrival he prophesied would happen spontaneously, as a result of inexorable transformations hardwired into the very structure of capitalism itself, was one variation on a familiar theme. Followers of what was then often called Marxian socialism accordingly waited eagerly but passively for the revolution to arrive, rather than doing anything to bring it about.

That began to change in 1902 when an exiled Russian Marxist named Vladimir Ilyich Ulyanov, who wrote political essays in Switzerland under the pen name Lenin, published a pamphlet titled *What Is to Be Done?* In place of the inevitable play of economic forces on which Marx placed his Neptunian faith, Lenin called for a highly disciplined and secretive vanguard party, which would subvert the existing order of society, and make the revolution happen using Plutonian strategies. By the time the pamphlet appeared, Lenin was already involved in radical politics in the Russian émigré community in western Europe, and in 1903 he and his followers took effective control of the Russian Social Democratic Labor Party, the largest Russian radical party of the time. At the party congress that year, at which Lenin's group triumphed, his followers were the majority, *bolsheviki* in Russian; the label "Bolshevik" stuck.

Over the decades that followed, he developed his theory of revolution, found allies in Russia and abroad, took an active role in the rough-and-tumble of Russian radical politics in exile, and waited for his chance. That chance came in 1917, when revolution broke out in Russia and the tsar was forced to abdicate. The First World War was raging and the direct route from Switzerland to Russia led straight through enemy territory, but Lenin convinced the German government to let him and his inner circle of followers through to St. Petersburg.

Once there he lost no time preparing for action. In October of 1917, Lenin staged a successful coup d'état—the "ten days that shook the world" of later Marxist legend—against the democratic government that had replaced the tsar. Once in power he and his followers established a government and tightened their control over the country in the years that followed, winning a civil war against Russian conservatives and driving off expeditionary forces sent by several other nations, including the United States. Conservatives around the world rolled their eyes and insisted that the newly founded Soviet Union would promptly collapse in humiliation due to its pie-in-the-sky economic theories. Radicals of a Neptunian bent, for their part, heaped uncritical praise on Lenin and his Communist Party, and heaped colorful fantasies onto the Russian experiment.

Neither side in those well-worn debates realized at first that something Marx had never envisaged was taking shape in the former Russian empire: a totalitarian police state where informers, secret police, mass graves, and prison camps became the norm. Even after Lenin died and Joseph Stalin took power, launching the first of a series of purges and mass murders that would kill thirty million Russian citizens, Neptunian radicals in the West continued to insist that the Soviet Union was a worker's paradise and the best hope of the future of humankind. Many of those radicals ended up spying for the Soviet Union in due time, as Pluto's subterranean influences pushed them toward secrecy and subversion.

By the time Pluto was discovered, communism was entrenched in the Soviet Union and communist parties loyal to Moscow had been founded in many other nations. A large, well-funded, and secretive organization, the Communist International, or Comintern, flooded the rest of the world with pro-Soviet propaganda and with spies and agents of influence. Subversive, violent, revolutionary, and for the moment triumphant, communism had embraced the Plutonian influence, and was hard at work splitting the world itself into communist and anticommunist halves, laying the foundations for the Cold War.

Psychoanalysis

As I hinted a little earlier in this chapter, the psychological revolution launched by Sigmund Freud had at least as much of an impact on society and culture as the scientific revolution launched by Albert Einstein. At the core of Freud's work was the recognition that most of the activities of the mind never broke through to the surface of consciousness. The concept of the unconscious mind was not original to Freud—it had in fact been introduced by a series of earlier psychologists over the course of the last three decades of the nineteenth century—but Freud showed more clearly than any of his predecessors how dreams, fantasies, slips of the tongue, and many other phenomena could best be understood as expressions of the unconscious mind, expressions of thoughts and desires that in many cases had been suppressed and deliberately forgotten by the conscious mind.

Late nineteenth-century European culture being what it was, nearly all those thoughts and desires linked up in one way or another with sex. An entire category of mental illnesses common among women in the Victorian era, called hysterical disorders in Freud's time and conversion disorders in ours, turned out to be curable in short order once their sexual basis was understood. The root of the problem was the same suppression of female sexuality that gave rise to the phantom moon Lilith: most women of the respectable classes were raised to believe that normal, healthy women never had sexual desires at all, and that if they themselves felt such desires, that demonstrated conclusively that they were depraved, unnatural creatures doomed to a life of shame, a miserable death, and eternal torment in the flames of hell.

Given such attitudes, it was quite common for middle-class women in Freud's time to respond to ordinary sexual feelings by becoming mentally unhinged. It was routine, for example, for teenage girls who succumbed to the temptation to masturbate to suffer thereafter from "glove anesthesia," a sudden paralysis of the hand they had used to stimulate themselves. It was even more common for women of any age who caught themselves feeling sexual desires toward someone to develop hysterical symptoms whenever they encountered some trigger that reminded them of the incident. The spread of Freudian psychology made such disorders much less common than they had been, and not just because Freudian therapy became a common social habit all over the industrial world. The mere fact that most literate people knew the basics of Freud's theories undercut the mechanism of repression. With the spread of popular knowledge concerning Freudian psychology, after all, by 1930 or so the general response to a case of glove anesthesia became, "Ah, I see that someone's been masturbating."

More broadly, the popularity of Freud's theories made it impossible to maintain the destructive fiction that respectable women had no sexual desires. Here Pluto functioned in his most positive aspect, cleaning out the Augean stables of the Western mind in a single explosive act. By the time Pluto was discovered, the Freudian revolution was in full flood, and pundits confidently predicted that in the years immediately ahead countless personal and social problems would be solved once and for all by the onward march of psychoanalysis.

It is worth noting that just as fission trumped fusion in the realm of nuclear power, *psychoanalysis*—the word literally means "taking apart the mind"—took center stage in the realm of early twentieth-century psychology, with little room left over for putting minds back together. The most famous psychological heretic of the era, Freud's erstwhile student Carl Jung, was able to find a niche market for his system, which had synthesis as its long-term goal but started by dividing the mind into even more parts than Freud did. Those systems of psychology that pursued the unification of the mind in any more direct way, such as Roberto Assagioli's system of psychosynthesis, were purely phenomena of the fringe while the Plutonian era lasted.

Modern Art

Among the most fascinating markers of the Plutonian era is the sudden transformation that seized art, architecture, and music around the time of Pluto's discovery. You have to read books on art published in or before the 1920s to grasp just how drastic a change happened in the early 1930s. In the usual way of such things, more recent works on art history have redefined the artistic movements of the past in the image of the present and given the precursors of modern and postmodern art a retrospective importance they did not have in their own time.

The great majority of the paintings produced by professional artists in the Western world in the decade or two prior to Pluto's discovery would have been comprehensible to Leonardo or Rembrandt—that is, they were attractive, skillfully rendered representations in paint of recognizable persons, scenes, and the like, intended to communicate a meaning to the broadest possible audience and also to appeal to the viewer's sense of beauty. Furthermore, the great majority of the paintings that won prizes in juried art shows and salons could be described in exactly these terms. Those few artistic factions of the time that rejected this approach, such as the Fauves, were fringe phenomena even in the art scene, and of essentially no interest to anyone outside it.

After 1930, however, the fringe became the center, and modern art became abstract, uncommunicative, and above all else, stunningly ugly. Representational art was rejected by critics and artists alike in favor of abstractions of various kinds, culminating in random splashes or patches of paint on canvases from which all meaning was deliberately erased. The cult of ugliness for its own sake became pervasive. Technical skill was increasingly neglected in favor of faux-primitive crudeness, and artists came to use "artist's statements" to explain works that were too ineptly fashioned to explain themselves. Then, as a capstone to the great pyramid of twentieth-century ugly art, the art scene witnessed the rise of celebrity poseurs such as Andy Warhol, whose works can best be described as elaborate practical jokes at the expense of the artistic establishment. With critical standards in complete disarray, and beauty and meaning considered irrelevant, such trickster figures had a field day: On what possible basis could anyone point out, for example, that a Campbell's soup label isn't a work of art?

The same thing happened in parallel in the fields of art, music, and architecture. In music, the heirs of Mozart and Beethoven abandoned the centuries-old language of tonality and harmony, the things that make music mean anything at all to the listener, and produced scores so discordant and incomprehensible that, as the joke goes, symphonies play pieces by living composers when they no longer want to put up with the inconvenience of having an audience. Some composers embraced various abstract schemes for structuring their pieces, twelve-tone technique and serialism among them, while others wove random sounds into their compositions. In these and other ventures into the realm of noise, the results were nearly always simply unlistenable. As with visual art, put-ons reigned supreme as the Plutonian era reached its zenith. The classic example is John Cage's famous 1952 piece *4'33"*, which consists entirely of rests—the musicians sit there doing nothing for the four minutes and thirty-three seconds of the piece and the "music" consists entirely of the background sounds of the auditorium. Absurd though this is, it is far and away the least unpleasant piece of music Cage ever wrote.

Architecture proceeded down a parallel path. Pre-Plutonian archi-tecture, brilliantly creative as it so often was, still stayed in contact with its own history and with the needs and wants of the people who lived and worked in it. After 1930 those practical concerns went straight out the plate-glass window. Led first by avant-garde figures such as Frank Lloyd Wright and Le Corbusier, and then taken worldwide by the celebrity architects of the International Style, architects competed with one another to produce stark, dysfunctional, dehumanizing, and monumentally ugly buildings. The Plutonian fixation on sexuality was as clearly evident in this field as in space travel; cities across the world accordingly sprouted skyscrapers that might best be described as huge erect penises made of concrete, glass, and steel—or perhaps as a series of gargantuan middle fingers extended toward those who had to live and work in or near them.

None of this was accidental. The flight into intentional ugliness that reduced painting, music, architecture, and other fine art forms into cari-catures of their former glory was driven by a schism just as significant, in its own way, as the splitting of the atom, the shattering of the psyche into quarreling fragments, the launching of human beings off the surface of the Earth, or the division of the world into communist and capitalist blocs. The schism in question? The opening up of the widest possible gap between artist and audience. Before 1930 or so, outside of fringe movements like the ones noted above, what made an artwork successful was its ability to communicate ideas and emotions to the widest possible audience. After 1930, by contrast, what made an artwork successful was its ability to exclude as many people as possible from whatever ideas and emotions, if any, the artist might have concealed in it.

The impact of this shift is almost impossible to overstate. In the late nineteenth century, the opening of a big art show or the premiere of a new opera counted as a major public event, drawing attention from the mass media of the day, and attracting an audience from all walks of life. By the late twentieth century, by contrast, the opening of a big art show or the premiere of a new opera had become the recherché concern of a tiny if well-funded subculture, whose members as often as not preened themselves over their ability to extract morsels of meaning and enjoyment out of creations that had been designed to make any such extraction as difficult and unrewarding as possible.

These are merely the most obvious forms that the influence of Pluto took in the opening decades of the Plutonian era. There were many others, and readers who take the time to reflect on Pluto's symbolism will have no difficulty naming a good many of them. In all its forms, as noted in the introduction to this book, the potent influences of the new planet expressed themselves in the form of *opposition to cosmos*.

The word *cosmos* comes from ancient Greek and means "that which is beautifully ordered." The word *cosmetic* derives from the same root. In the vast majority of human societies this is how the universe is perceived—a beautifully ordered whole system—and every aspect of human culture in these societies strives, successfully or otherwise, to emulate that order and its beauty. This is why the political institutions, social arrangements, landscape planning, arts, and architecture of so many traditional societies are deliberately modeled on the structure of the universe as each society understands it. Human affairs, from this perspective, thrive best when they are consciously understood as inseparable parts of a greater cosmos, attuned to the ordered beauty of the heavens and the earth.

This was the vision of humanity and the universe that went into eclipse during the Plutonian era. In its place rose a vision of humanity as a stranger in a hostile and meaningless universe. Iconic weird-fantasy writer H. P. Lovecraft, whose most famous stories were all written during a period that opened a few years before the discovery of Pluto and closed a few years after, caught the flavor of that vision more perfectly, perhaps, than any other author, in the opening lines of his story "The Call of Cthulhu."

> The most merciful thing in the world, I think, is the inability of the human mind to correlate all its contents. We live on a placid isle of ignorance in the midst of black seas of infinity, and it was not meant that we should voyage far. The sciences, each straining in its own direction, have hitherto harmed us little; but someday the piecing together of dissociated knowledge will open up such terrifying vistas of reality, and of our frightful position therein, that we shall either go mad from the revelation or flee from the deadly light into the peace and safety of a new dark age.

Much the same sentiment, expressed in even more uncompromising terms, came from the pen of British philosopher Bertrand Russell in his 1903 essay "A Free Man's Worship."

> That Man is the product of causes which had no prevision of the end they were achieving; that his origin, his growth, his hopes and fears, his loves and his beliefs, are but the outcome of accidental collocations of atoms; that no fire, no heroism, no intensity of thought and feeling, can preserve an individual life beyond the grave; that all the labors of the ages, all the devotion, all the inspiration, all the noonday brightness of human genius, are destined to extinction in the vast death of the solar system, and that the whole temple of Man's achievement must inevitably be buried beneath the debris of a universe in ruins—all these things, if not quite beyond dispute,

are yet so nearly certain, that no philosophy which rejects them can hope to stand. Only within the scaffolding of these truths, only on the firm foundation of unyielding despair, can the soul's habitation henceforth be safely built.

This was the Plutonian vision of human existence. To Lovecraft, Russell, and countless other people during the first half of the Plutonian era, this was reality. To them, the vision of cosmos, the beautiful order that guided the lives of countless generations in the great cultures of the past, could never be anything but the delusion of primitive minds; to them, modernity meant above all the embrace of their cold vision, and that vision would continue to rule our lives forever unless the peace and comfort of a new dark age, in Lovecraft's ironic phrasing, lifted the burden from us for a while, or until the extinction of our species finished the job.

There was, however, one difficulty with these confident pronouncements. It was a difficulty they shared with the equally confident pronouncements that nuclear power would replace all other energy sources with limitless electricity too cheap to meter, that nuclear weapons would either force world peace at last or wipe us all out, that Freudian psychoanalysis would transform the individual and society forever, that communism was the inevitable wave of the future, and so on through the litany of grand proclamations that played so large and public a role in Pluto's heyday. All of these, as the Plutonian era drew on, turned out to be wildly overblown—and even the foundation of despair on which Russell proposed to build a habitation for the human soul turned out to be much less unyielding than he thought.

SIX

The Twilight of Pluto

The trouble began, as any old-fashioned astrologer could have predicted, with the planet Pluto itself, and the first whispers of it could be heard very nearly as soon as Pluto received its name and became the public's darling. The spokespeople and publicists of the scientific establishment didn't worry about such things; they were quick to set the discovery of Pluto alongside those of Uranus and Neptune as one more triumph of rationality. They didn't mention that Ceres had spent fifty years as a planet, of course—you can read a remarkable number of modern books on the history of astronomy without ever learning about that. As Charles Fort pointed out a long time ago, the reputation of science has been laboriously constructed over the years by crowing endlessly about its successes while sweeping its many failures under the nearest available rug. In all the enthusiasm over Pluto's discovery, it was easy to lose track of one small but critical detail: the new planet didn't make the solar system's mathematics work any better than they had before.

The earliest estimates of Pluto's mass, back when it was still Planet X, calculated that it was another big planet like Uranus or Neptune, because a smaller planet would not exert enough gravitational force to cause the anomalies in the orbits of Uranus and Neptune that the unknown planet was intended to explain. Percival Lowell's own estimate, made in 1915, gauged Planet X as roughly seven times the mass of Earth, which was small by outer planet standards but still a very substantial world.

The planet discovered by Tombaugh was so far from the Sun that it could only be sighted as a pinpoint of light. Any direct estimate of its size had to wait for a space program capable of lofting telescopes into orbit and sending space probes to take close-up snapshots, so the scientists of the 1930s had to rely in indirect means, none of them foolproof. The first guesses based on those indirect indications, immediately after the discovery, nonetheless gave Pluto a much smaller mass, more or less equal to Earth's. That was a problem, because a body only as massive as Earth didn't exert enough gravity to put the necessary wobble in the orbits of Uranus and Neptune. It was a problem only for scientists, however, and popular culture adapted without difficulty to an Earth-sized Pluto.

For the scientists worse was to follow. One of the better indirect ways to gauge a distant planet's size is to keep a telescope trained on it while it passes in front of a star. Measure how long the star's light is blocked by the planet, factor in the planet's distance and speed, and you've got a yardstick of fair sensitivity. As astronomers used that method repeatedly on Pluto, their best guesses of its size and mass shrank steadily.

The detection of Pluto's largest moon, Charon, in 1978 put the icing on the cake. One of the many useful consequences of Isaac Newton's laws of planetary motion is that if you know the orbit and speed of a moon, you can tell the mass of the planet it orbits quite accurately; it's the cosmic equivalent of plopping a planet on a colossal bathroom scale. Once they had access to Charon's orbital data, scientists promptly figured out that Pluto was tiny, with a mass less than 1/400th that of Earth's, small enough that seven moons in the solar system are bigger—our own moon, for example, has seven times Pluto's mass. Pluto's trajectory as the incredible shrinking planet was so relentless that a tongue-in-cheek 1980 article in the astronomical journal *Eos* noted wryly that if current trends continued, Pluto would disappear entirely by 1984.

The alarming decrease in Pluto's mass launched several new searches for yet another Planet X, but there were several important reasons why those didn't attract much attention or find any results. The most important was that Clyde Tombaugh, having discovered Pluto less than a year after beginning his career as a professional astronomer, went on to spend the next thirteen years surveying a very large fraction of the sky for other planets. He found plenty of asteroids and other little bodies, but no Planet X.

Some astronomers suggested that Planet X was hiding in one of the corners of the sky Tombaugh didn't search, but nobody had much interest in taking the hunt further, and for good reason. In the days before modern computer technology automated the process, searching the far reaches of the solar system for distant planets was one of the most tedious tasks in all of science. It was done with a clever device called a blink comparator, which holds two photographs of the same small piece of sky that were taken at two different times and allows you to switch from one to the other very quickly. If something changes position slightly when one photograph gives way to another, you know you've spotted a comet, an asteroid, or (just maybe) a new planet. Imagine spending eight hours a day, five days a week, for years at a time, loading photos into a blink comparator and flipping from one image to the other, and you'll soon realize why it wasn't a popular activity!

As it turned out, though, the entire quest for another Planet X was based on a misconception, or more precisely a mismeasurement. In 1993, using the far more precise data on planetary masses made possible by the Voyager space probe missions, astrophysicist E. Myles Standish Jr. showed that Planet X was entirely an artifact of inaccurate measurements. Plug the Voyager-derived figures for planetary masses and orbits into Newton's equations, in other words, and Uranus, Neptune, and all the other planets do exactly what they're supposed to do in response to each other's gravity and that of the Sun. Planet X accordingly vanished like the phantom it always was. Curiously, unlike Vulcan and Lilith, Planet X never seems to have developed a post-Plutonian character of its own; whatever influence it might have represented seems never to have surfaced far enough to become a presence in our collective consciousness.

Meanwhile, while Pluto shrank inexorably and the phantom of Planet X haunted the imaginations of astronomers, popular books on astronomy were backing quietly away from the claim that Pluto was a planet after all. In 1962, when Time-Life Books published David Bergamini's highly readable and gorgeously illustrated *The Universe* as part of the bestselling Life Nature series, Pluto appeared in its usual place as the ninth planet, though Bergamini prudently noted what were then growing doubts about its proper status. By 1985, when the same publishing firm released Kendrick Frazier's equally readable and gorgeously illustrated *Solar System* as part of its Planet Earth series, Pluto is stuck in at the end of a chapter otherwise devoted to the gas giants of the outer solar system, and Frazier noted that the little iceball "barely deserves planetary status," and that some scientists wanted it reclassified as a minor body.

In 2006, as recounted in the introduction, those scientists got their wish. Once the painfully slow process of sorting through images of the sky two at a time with a blink comparator could be replaced by high-speed computer systems running digital searches through vast data banks of celestial images, the first of Pluto's many comrades in the Kuiper Belt showed up promptly. As soon as Pluto was assigned to its proper role in the solar system, it settled just as promptly into its new status as the only Kuiper Belt object big enough and close enough to the Sun to be spotted by non-digital means. Like Ceres before it, Pluto had finished its career as a planet, and its 2006 demotion marked the beginning of the end of the Plutonian era.

An important difference sets Pluto apart from the other former planets we've discussed, however. When Ceres was quietly demoted from planet to asteroid, no one protested, and when Einstein proved that Vulcan had never existed in the first place, there were no letter-writing campaigns insisting that it be put back into the roster of planets. The popular uproar that emerged in response to Pluto's downgrading was unprecedented and, from an astrological standpoint, fascinating. Popular culture is just as strongly influenced by astrological factors as, say, the decisions of astronomical organizations, and so Pluto's role as a pop-culture darling deserves close attention. This is all the more significant in that the response to Pluto's decline and demotion within the astrological community was indistinguishable from that of popular culture as a whole.

THE TWILIGHT OF PLUTO IN ASTROLOGY

It's an irony of no small proportion that the downgrading of Pluto took most astrologers completely by surprise. While astronomers discussed the dwindling estimates of Pluto's mass and laid the foundations for the decision in 2006, and (as we'll see) many of the most distinctive phenomena of the Plutonian era declined at roughly the same pace, astrologers by and large went blithely on their way treating Pluto as a planet, making predictions that assumed it would continue to retain its planetary status forever. Once the downgrade happened, in turn, many people in the astrological community insisted indignantly, right along with their astrologically ignorant neighbors, that Pluto certainly was a planet, and the astronomers didn't know what they were talking about. There were reasons for that blindness to the signs of the times, reasons with deep roots in the recent history of astrology. It's worth taking a moment to glance at those reasons to see why the arrival of so important a change was missed, and then resisted, by those who ought to have been more attentive to it than anyone else.

Until the early decades of the twentieth century, the astrology practiced in most Western countries still embraced attitudes and habits of thought that had been central to astrological practice since ancient Greek times. Among the most important of these was the recognition that the influences of the heavens can impose sharp limits on our freedom to do whatever we want. Those influences aren't omnipotent and their limits are correspondingly flexible in certain ways—as an old astrological adage has it, "the stars incline, they do not compel"—but until the Plutonian era astrologers and their clients alike understood that among the things that can be learned from a birth chart are which of the client's hopes and dreams will never be fulfilled, which parts of their lives will always be sources of trouble and frustration, which of their desires should be put on indefinite hold because trying to fulfill them will inevitably prove to be a bad idea, and so on.

After the discovery of Pluto, especially but not only in the United States, such counsels became highly unfashionable. A new generation of astrologers and astrological writers, of whom Marc Edmund Jones and Dane Rudhyar were the most influential, reworked astrology to focus on psychology rather than prediction: in effect, answering the question "Who am I?" rather than the more traditional astrological question "What will life bring to me?"—while tacitly avoiding the hard questions about limits and difficulties that the older forms of astrology explored so well. The resulting personality-centered approach to astrology became immensely popular in the astrological community, and when astrology found a mass audience again in the wake of the 1960s counterculture, that was the astrology that most people adopted.

On its own terms, personality-centered astrology is a worthy addition to the astrological toolkit, and a birth chart drawn up and delineated with that approach in mind can be a valuable tool for self-knowledge and psychotherapy. It's an open secret among historians of Jungian psychology, for example, that the famous Swiss psychotherapist Carl Jung was a capable astrologer and used horoscopes of his patients to guide their therapy. However useful personality-centered astrology is, it posed a downside—those modes of astrology that didn't focus on individual psychology fell into temporary eclipse during its heyday. In particular, mundane astrology—the astrology of nations, peoples, and great historical cycles—suffered more than its share of neglect during the twentieth century.

That neglect was never total; a handful of astrologers kept using traditional mundane methods to make political predictions: for example, ingress charts, which are drawn up for the solstices and equinoxes over political capitals, and grand conjunctions, charts defined by the conjunctions of Jupiter and Saturn, which mark the beginning of new epochs in world history. Even among the few, however, the personality-centered approach made substantial inroads, and many of the resulting predictions thus focused on changes in popular moods and collective psychology rather than, say, the risks of war or the vagaries of the economy.

To be fair, there was a rather more specific reason why classic mundane astrology fell into eclipse in the middle years of the twentieth century. In the spring of 1939, a group of British astrologers led by the eminent C. E. O. Carter issued a ringing proclamation—based on their interpretation of the Aries ingress chart for 1939—that war would not happen that year. As history records, they were disastrously wrong, and the total failure of their prediction brought classic mundane astrology into serious disrepute.* The Second World War, which began that year, turned out to be the most destructive conflict ever waged by our species, and in its wake a method of prediction that failed to anticipate so vast a struggle attracted very little interest.

The eclipse of mundane astrology had another effect, though, that bears upon our theme. The discovery or downgrading of a planet is above all a consideration in mundane astrology. As we've seen, the discovery of a previously unknown planet marks the appearance of a new factor in human history and culture, while the demotion or disproof of a supposed planet represents the fading out of a factor that has had its day. A few astrological writers—notably Richard Tarnas in *Cosmos and Psyche*—have explored the implications of the discovery of a planet, but I know of none who has glanced back at the histories of Ceres, Vulcan, and the dark moon Lilith and thought about what it

---

*This is not the place to discuss why their prediction was so badly mistaken. I will show in a future book that they misread obvious indications of war because of their own political prejudices.

would mean if another supposed planet was stricken from the list. Nor did the handful of active mundane astrologers pay attention either to the steady decline in estimates of Pluto's mass, on the one hand, or the equally steady decline in the importance of those historical phenomena that most clearly expressed the Plutonian influence.

Of course, there was a broader astrological context to the new personality-centered astrology. The fixation on the individual and the eclipse of the idea that astrological influences limited personal freedom was another expression of that core theme of the Plutonian era, the rejection of cosmos. Among the consequences of living in an ordered cosmos are, first, the sobering recognition that human beings can desire things that they cannot achieve, and second, the equally unwelcome knowledge that human beings can desire and achieve things that will reliably blow up in their faces. A great deal of the personality-centered astrology of the Plutonian era did its best to avoid those insights. Thus, it's not surprising that so many astrologers of the time, deeply committed as they were to the personality-centered approach, clung to the planet that appeared to give them the freedom to ignore the unwelcome realities inseparable from an ordered cosmos.

THE TWILIGHT OF PLUTO IN HISTORY

While these attitudes remained fixed in place among astrologers, the decline of Pluto and of the Plutonian influence unfolded steadily. Among the most remarkable things about the Plutonian era, in fact, was neatly summarized by the very Plutonian poet T. S. Eliot in 1925: so many of the things that came in with a bang during the first half or so of that era went out with a whimper in the second half. During the waning years of its influence, in fact, Pluto might best be described as the planet of failed promises and overblown hype, the ruler of all of the many loudly ballyhooed waves of the future that so reliably proceeded to break and flow back out to sea.

Yet that waning passed unnoticed by an astonishing number of people. The astrologers who missed the twilight of Pluto were more than matched by the people who clung to other manifestations of the Plutonian current long after those had passed their peak and obviously failed to live up to the promises made for them. Like the schoolchildren who demanded that Pluto be restored to a place among the planets it no longer deserved by any astronomical measure, a great many people clung to Plutonian visions of the future long after any objective assessment of those visions would have guaranteed them a place in history's scrapheap.

✦

Nuclear Fission

Pluto's twilight can be seen with unusual clarity in the history of nuclear fission after 1945. The atomic bombs that incinerated Hiroshima and Nagasaki and brought a sudden stop to the Second World War shook the world in more than a literal sense. Millions of people realized overnight that the end of the world was no longer a purely theological concept, and the fear of nuclear war became steadily more widespread as the United States and the Soviet Union vied with one another to stockpile ever larger numbers of nuclear weapons and build and deploy more robust and unstoppable delivery systems. American schoolchildren in the 1950s and 1960s accordingly went through regular "duck and cover" drills at school, meant to teach them to shield themselves from the effects of a nuclear blast. A good many of those schoolchildren—most of the baby boom generation, in fact—spent a large part of their youthful years convinced that a nuclear war was inevitable, and they would never live to see adulthood.

Meanwhile the hope that nuclear power could also be used to generate electricity in vast amounts at low cost led to massive programs of nuclear power plant construction in most of the world's industrial nations. The idea that fossil fuels would soon be phased out, replaced by clean, safe, and almost infinitely abundant electricity from nuclear power plants, was all over the media of the time, and not just among cheerleaders for industry. The visionary architect Paolo Soleri, for example, who invented the concept of arcologies—gargantuan structures that contained entire cities in a single building—assumed as a matter of course that each arcology would have a nuclear power plant in its basement, turning out as much power as the arcology's inhabitants could possibly want.

Caught between the terror of nuclear war and the promise of nuclear power, many people at that time saw nuclear fission as the keynote of their time, and it was fashionable to claim that the mushroom cloud over Hiroshima marked a major—perhaps *the* major—turning point in human history. Whether we were all doomed to perish in nuclear war or could count on limitless electrical power as the normal birthright of every human being once the bugs got worked out of fission-reactor technology, it was—or looked like—a nuclear age.

As it turned out, though, the terror and the promise both rested on foundations of empty air. The threat of nuclear warfare gradually receded as military planners in all the nuclear powers discovered to their chagrin that no matter how they crunched the numbers, the only way to win a nuclear war was to stay out of it. When the economic consequences of a single nuclear explosion over a large city would make it the greatest single catastrophe in any nation's history, and the impact of ten such explosions would cause any country in the world to cease to exist as a viable national community, justifications for pushing the button became impossible to find. The world's nuclear powers thus settled willy-nilly into a posture of mutually assured destruction. Even when a major nuclear power underwent political collapse, as happened to the Soviet Union in 1991, the missiles stayed safely in their silos and the bombers sat unused in their hangars.

Meanwhile, nuclear power turned out to be even less viable in the longer run than nuclear weapons. The problem it faced was not technical in nature, it was economic. Whenever cost was no object—as in the case of the nuclear vessels of the United States Navy—nuclear reactors proved to be sturdy and reliable sources of power. Take the same technology and put it on the market in competition with other modes of power, however, and it becomes a black hole into which endless amounts of money had to be poured. That was what happened to the NS *Savannah,* the first nuclear-powered freighter, which entered service in 1959. Technically she was an impressive triumph, but in economic terms she was a dismal flop; she cost on average $2 million a year more to operate than a comparable freighter powered by diesel engines, and she ended up being deactivated and mothballed in 1971. Only three other nuclear-powered cargo ships were built, and they also turned out to be vastly uneconomical white elephants. Not one of them is still in service.

The same thing happened on an even bigger scale with nuclear power plants. While the cheerleading rhetoric of the 1950s claimed that nuclear power would produce electricity too cheap to meter, the reality was that it produced electricity too expensive to pay for itself. No nation on Earth has ever been able to establish a nuclear power industry without huge and ongoing government subsidies. Nuclear accidents at Three-Mile Island, Chernobyl, and Fukushima Daiichi got all the press, but the disaster that doomed nuclear power was the financial collapse of the Washington Public Power Supply System (WPPSS), unaffectionately remembered by many people in the Pacific Northwest as "Whoops!" When its ambitious program of nuclear power plant construction turned into an economic belly flop and forced it to default on its bonds in 1982, that dealt a body blow to the nuclear industry from which it has never recovered. Over the years since then, the number of new nuclear power plants under construction has steadily dwindled, and cost overruns have caused a great many of those started to be abandoned before completion.

The Plutonian themes of failed promises and overblown hype became a constant theme in discussions of nuclear power as the industry entered its ongoing decline. Every few years since the dawn of nuclear power, some new version of nuclear power technology—breeder reactors, thorium reactors, molten salt reactors, small modular reactors, and the list goes on—has been proclaimed as the solution to the industry's problems and the energy source of the future. None of them get far, because none of them offer a solution to the brutal economic realities of nuclear power, and technical feasibility means nothing if your technology can't pay its own costs.

The same is even more true, of course, of fusion power. Despite generations of hard work by some of the world's best physicists, and endlessly repeated claims that fusion reactors will be viable any day now, practical fusion power remains an unsolved problem. What is more, the sheer cost of experimental reactors such as the ITER project in Switzerland make it painfully clear that even if the technical problems can be solved, fusion power will be even more hopelessly unaffordable than fission power. Though millions of dollars a year keep being poured down a succession of high-tech rat holes, due to a combination of institutional inertia and the waning but still potent prestige of science, the writing is on the wall for fusion.

Space Travel

Those of my readers who grew up in what were assumed to be the opening years of the Space Age, as I did, will remember the curious way that humanity's grand march into space drifted to an awkward halt over the course of the 1970s. From 1957, when *Sputnik I* went into orbit and proved to an astonished world that spaceflight was no longer limited to the pages of pulp science fiction magazines, the pace of innovation was rapid: *Vostok* and *Mercury,* the pioneering one-man capsules fielded by the Soviet Union and the United States respectively, gave way to the larger *Voskhod* and *Gemini* capsules, and then to the sturdy workhorses of the late 1960s, the *Soyuz* and *Apollo* spacecraft. Six successful Apollo missions left bootprints on the Moon; the first space station, the Soviet Union's *Salyut I,* was followed by six other Salyut stations and by the United States' Skylab. Meanwhile both nations sent a flurry of unmanned probes to the other planets of the solar system and plans for the first manned interplanetary missions were on the drawing boards.

Those never happened. By the 1980s most U.S. funding for

spaceflight was diverted into Earth satellites, the Space Shuttle, and the development of what became the International Space Station. The Soviet Union had already quietly scrapped its plans for a manned lunar landing in 1974. The future history envisioned by science fiction writers and fans, in which the first trip to the Moon would inevitably be followed by flights to Mars and the other planets, suddenly ground to a halt. After the Apollo 17 Moon landing in 1972, manned space travel was quietly restricted to low Earth orbit.

There was a very good reason for that change of plans, though it takes careful reading of the published literature about interplanetary space to figure out what it was. There turned out to be a difficulty with space travel that no one had anticipated—outside Earth's protective magnetosphere, the solar system is flooded with torrents of hard radiation from the vast unshielded thermonuclear reactor we call the Sun. No other potentially habitable planet in the solar system, it turned out, has a magnetosphere like the Earth's to protect its surface from radiation. Worse, while it takes only around three days of spaceflight to reach the Moon, going to Mars would require a flight some nine months long, all of it spent soaking up the Sun's output of hard radiation, to reach a planet without a protective magnetosphere—and then, of course, there would be the flight back.

As interplanetary space probes brought back high radiation readings all through the 1970s, space scientists and the bureaucrats who managed them found themselves in an unenviable situation. With the help of media spectacles such as *Star Trek* and *Star Wars,* the dream of humanity's future in space had become so solidly rooted in the popular imagination that no one dared come out and challenge it directly. Fortunately, the War on Poverty, the War on Cancer, the Global War on Terror, and similar exercises in politically necessary futility have taught government employees a great deal about the fine art of going through the motions of programs that will never accomplish their purported goals. That same form of maneuvering became the central activity of NASA and its equivalents overseas as the years passed.

When Pluto began its descent from planetary status, the number of countries with active space programs hit an all-time high, but nearly all of those focused sensibly on the services that satellites can provide to people here on Earth. China, Russia, and the United States kept manned spaceflight programs running, all strictly limited to low orbits well within the protective blanket of the magnetosphere, and the International Space Station continued to orbit in the same safe zone. The dream of human colonization of other worlds still got an extensive workout as a vehicle for propaganda in the media and the political sphere, but technical challenges to any such project piled up steadily, and by the end of the millennium it became clear to clear-sighted observers that the Space Age was winding down.

Communism

The decades immediately following the discovery of Pluto saw communism reach its zenith. In 1945 the Soviet Union defeated Nazi Germany, its sole significant European rival, and imposed communist governments on the nations of Eastern Europe. In 1949 China's long civil war ended with communist leader Mao Zedong in control of the world's most populous nation. All through the 1950s and 1960s, communist parties were significant forces in the political climate across Europe and much of the Third World, while communist insurgencies flared in more than twenty countries. Meanwhile, the Soviet space program leaped ahead of the United States, launching the first satellite, putting the first man in orbit, and sending probes to other planets while the United States desperately tried to play catch-up. It really did look as though communism was on its way to world domination.

Then, in lockstep with other manifestations of Pluto's influence, the communist juggernaut began to falter. The United States, not the Soviet Union, put the first human bootprints on the Moon, and took the lead in crucial new economic sectors such as computer technology and genetic engineering, while the Soviet Union began to sink into stagnation and malaise. That worsened after 1981, when the Reagan administration launched a brilliantly successful program of economic warfare, crashing the price of oil to deprive the Soviet Union of its main source of hard currency, and triggering a series of hugely expensive arms races that the United States could afford but the Soviet Union ultimately could not.

The ultimate weakness of the communist system, curiously enough, turned out to be the same as the ultimate weakness of nuclear power: economics. The socialist economic system devised by Karl Marx was after all the pet theory of an intellectual who had little if any contact with the gritty realities of supply and demand—in astrological terms, a perfect expression of the less helpful end of Neptune's influence— and it simply didn't work when put to the test of everyday life. While the capitalist nations after the Second World War saw consumer goods proliferate and standards of living soar, the communist world remained locked into a grim round of economic dysfunction in which even the most basic consumer products were not always available, and political repression alone kept the faltering system together.

Finally, not even the apparatuses of secret police and prison camps could prop up a failing system. In 1989 the Berlin Wall came down and the communist governments of Eastern Europe promptly collapsed. In 1991 the Soviet Union disintegrated and the Communist Party fell from power in Russia. In the years that followed, China quietly shelved its official Marxist economic theory and replaced it with a hybrid economy in which private enterprise and state-owned corporations coexisted in an uneasy relationship. By the time Pluto was downgraded from planetary status, a movement that had shaken the world ninety years prior was settling quietly into place in history's dustbin.

Psychoanalysis

By the middle decades of the twentieth century, as other manifestations of the Plutonian era peaked, the psychological revolution set in motion by Sigmund Freud reached its zenith. It wasn't simply that Freudian psychotherapy had become the default approach to psychological care in many Western countries, though this was true, or that Freud's ideas about sexuality and the unconscious mind were widely accepted among professionals in the field, though this was true as well. Psychoanalysis had also become a huge cultural force. Getting psychoanalyzed had become a common habit among the intelligentsia and the more cultured end of the well-to-do. Novels on Freudian themes, such as Philip Roth's *Portnoy's Complaint,* streamed forth in impressive numbers by big publishing houses, and some of them became bestsellers. Films and live theater followed suit, with wildly successful productions such as 1969's musical revue *Oh! Calcutta* focusing entirely on sexuality seen through a Freudian lens.

Meanwhile, under the influence of Freud's theories, popular attitudes toward sex made a dramatic U-turn. Leading thinkers of the 1950s and 1960s such as Norman O. Brown and Herbert Marcuse denounced sexual repression with the same enthusiasm, and in much the same tones, that their grandparents had denounced sexual licentiousness. Writers of popular fiction and nonfiction followed their lead. An entire literature of sexual utopianism, of which Robert A. Heinlein's bestselling science fiction novel *Stranger in a Strange Land* is a typical example, extolled the marvelous new world of orgiastic happiness and perfect sanity that would arrive just as soon as the last scraps of Victorian morality were swept away, and everybody started behaving like minks in mating season. Finally, the development of the birth control pill finished the job that Freud started, sharply decreasing the risk of accidental pregnancy. Within months of its release to the public, the Sexual Revolution was on.

Yet the utopia of free love and sexual liberation envisioned by Brown and Marcuse, and portrayed so colorfully by Heinlein and his peers, never managed to live up to the expectations loaded so enthusiastically onto it. While it's true that conversion disorders became much less common than they were in Freud's day, other psychological problems took their place. A society of compulsive sexual hyperactivity turned out to have just as many downsides as a society of compulsive sexual repression—among other things, sexual harassment and pedophilia became even more significant social problems than they had been, as the "anything goes" attitude toward sexual mores gave an assortment of predators plenty of room to operate without interference. By the end of the twentieth century, the longing for a less overwhelmingly hypersexualized society had become a potent political and cultural force in many countries.

As Pluto shrank, in turn, so did interest in Freud's theories. Part of the problem was simply that the Freudian revolution succeeded too well, and the cultural changes it set in motion made the neuroses Freudian therapy can cure much less common than they had been. Part of the problem was that psychotherapists generally were early adopters of the "disease management" model of medicine, in which health care professionals manage illnesses instead of curing them: a highly lucrative arrangement for the health care industry, to be sure, but patients faced with endless bills and no cure in sight increasingly went elsewhere. Another part of the problem was competition from the pharmaceutical industry, which pushed its own drug-based therapies for mental conditions in a largely successful attempt to expand its own market share at the expense of drug-free therapies such as Freudian psychoanalysis.

Yet the core problem with Freud's theories is that they simply didn't stand up to scientific testing, critical analysis, or the assessment of patients who wanted help with their emotional problems. Experimental evidence backing Freudian theory and therapy proved to be extremely hard to find; in fact, a 2004 study by INSERM, the French National Institute for Health and Medical Research, determined that Freudian therapy was significantly *less* effective than other forms of psychiatric treatment surveyed. Meanwhile, research into Freud's biography and writings turned up evidence of potential scientific fraud on his part. By 2015 the popularity of Freudian psychoanalysis had declined so far that psychoanalyst Bradley Peterson was quoted in an article in the *New York Times Magazine* saying, "I think most people would agree that psychoanalysis as a form of treatment is on its last legs."

Modern Art

For modern art, the last of the core Plutonian phenomena tracked in these pages, the course of decline followed much the same trajectory as psychoanalysis. In the middle decades of the twentieth century, as Pluto's influence reached its peak, leading artists and composers belonged to the celebrity class. Those colorful poseurs Andy Warhol and John Cage attracted the same kind of mass media attention as Hollywood starlets and aspiring national politicians and being able to follow the latest trends in art had a definite cachet in the cocktail circuit. Still, that popularity turned out to be a temporary phenomenon. Thereafter, without anyone ever quite getting around to saying anything about it, the avant-garde art and music scene slid into obscurity and irrelevance.

None of the changes that followed affected the fine art and art music scenes in any outward way. Art schools and music conservatories continued to steer students toward the latest fashions and away from anything that might be seen as beautiful or meaningful by the general public. Well-funded government welfare programs such as the National Endowment for the Arts, and an assortment of less richly endowed private funding sources, bought enough of the resulting product to make up for faltering sales from galleries. By century's end most artists were expected to produce paintings and sculptures that were destined to go straight from the studio to the storerooms of minor museums, with a few weeks on display in galleries or temporary exhibits somewhere in the middle and the hope of a spot on a wall in some future exhibit hovering in the indefinite future. Composers, for their part, were expected to turn out musical pieces that would be played only once, in front of an audience consisting only of those luckless individuals who couldn't find an excuse to stay away, and then published as proof of their creators' qualifications as bona fide members of the avant-garde.

The result, of course, was that a great many first-rate creative talents abandoned the formerly prestigious fine arts for fields in which their abilities would not be wasted on such exercises in futility, leaving the field increasingly filled with the less gifted. Public interest in the arts waned accordingly, and the grandchildren of the people who flocked to see exhibits of paintings by Andy Warhol and Jackson Pollock very often cannot name a single currently active painter, sculptor, composer of art music, or practitioner of any of the other fine arts—can you? Faced with the widespread loss of interest in modern art and music, art museums, symphonies, and other institutions tasked with keeping the fine arts in the public eye engaged in increasingly frantic maneuvers to try to attract attention to anything made in the Plutonian era.

A local example is as useful here as any other. The Rhode Island School of Design (RISD) art museum in downtown Providence, a short bus ride from where I live, has arranged its galleries so that anyone who comes in through the main entrance has to pass through a gallery of modern pieces before reaching the art that visitors actually want to see—a transparent and frankly desperate attempt to get people to pay attention to modern works whether they want to do so or not. When that proved insufficient, pieces by modern artists were placed higgledy-piggledy in the other galleries. This was a bad move, as having a modern piece side by side with a classic painting from Europe or Japan or a classic sculpture from ancient Egypt or West Africa shows with painful clarity just how ugly and ineptly fashioned the modern works are. Along the same lines, many orchestras have taken to inserting modern music in concerts that also feature baroque and classical pieces. They have learned from experience, however, that the modern pieces have to be played in the first half of the program. Otherwise, nearly all the attendees simply walk out the doors at the intermission.

Public architecture was the one exception to the general slide of the modern arts into oblivion, and it was an exception purely because public input was so systematically excluded from decisions concerning the built environment. Federal, state, and local officials provided the funding, celebrity architects came up with the plans, and everyone else simply had to live with the stunningly ugly and dysfunctional results. A similar dynamic played itself out in many of the larger religious denominations. In his aptly titled book *Ugly as Sin,* for example,

Roman Catholic architectural critic Michael Rose has documented how modernist clergy and celebrity architects went out of their way to commission and build new churches that were as hideous to look at as they were poorly suited for Catholic worship. As the Plutonian era began to wind down, the backlash against ugly architecture had yet to attain any degree of organizational strength or public exposure.

✦

Something else, however, was going on behind the scenes as the Plutonian era peaked and started in on its inexorable decline. The foundations of despair on which Russell tried to found human existence turned out to be much more brittle than he and his fellow materialists thought. That allowed the concept of cosmos, of a beautiful order uniting the individual and the universe, to begin to slip back in through the cracks.

Of course this started first on the fringes. One place where it became evident early on was in astrology itself. Beginning in the 1990s the domination of the field by the psychological approach began to fray as a new movement of traditional astrologers emerged. What set this new movement apart from their peers in the astrological circuit was that they insisted on using older forms of astrology—ancient Hellenistic, medieval Arabian, or European Renaissance methods—in place of the methods that Rudhyar, Jones, and their peers had introduced. The rejection of modern astrology often took dogmatic forms; for example, it was quite common for traditional astrologers to refuse to include Uranus, Neptune, and Pluto in their horoscopes at all. That rigidity was necessary, at least at first, so that the traditional astrologers could clear away the whole body of modern astrological practice and refocus attention away from personality and toward prediction.

Inevitably, disputes between modern and traditional astrologers flared, especially in those corners of the internet devoted to astrology. In the usual way of such things, these produced much more heat than light. Over time, though, a growing number of astrologers have begun to draw on elements of both systems, moving away from the strictly psychological approach while still making use of its techniques where these are appropriate. From these ventures, over the decades and centuries to come, the mature astrology of the post-Plutonian era will emerge.

Another phenomenon of the cultural fringes that showed the first stirrings of the rebirth of cosmos was the revival of sacred geometry—the tradition, dating back to Pythagoras, of using geometry as a spiritual discipline and a source of symbolism. The study of sacred geometry is rooted in the concept of *cosmos,* for the beautiful order that shapes all things is revealed with unusual clarity in the way that geometrical patterns unfold from simple beginnings. From ancient times this made the study of sacred geometry an important part of training in the inner spiritual traditions of the Western world, and it remained an important part of Western occultism through the Renaissance and the early stages of the scientific era.

Of all the branches of the Western occult tradition, accordingly, sacred geometry suffered the most complete eclipse during the heyday of the Plutonian era. The extraordinary work done by such writers as Jay Hambidge and Matila Ghyka, as recently as the 1920s, dropped into near-total obscurity once Pluto was discovered, and only a handful of little-known figures such as R. A. Schwaller de Lubicz kept the traditions of sacred geometry alive. That began to change in 1982 when Robert Lawlor's *Sacred Geometry: Philosophy and Practice* saw print, introducing some of the basic elements of Schwaller de Lubicz's work to a wider public. In the years that followed, an initial trickle of works on sacred geometry turned into a flood, and many of the classic works on the subject were republished for the first time in many decades.

More broadly, traditional Western occultism in general staged a remarkable comeback as the Plutonian era waned. The longing for the experience of cosmos in the waning years of Pluto took many forms, of course. The passage of Neptune, the planet of modern occultism, through the signs of the zodiac played a large role in that—those who were around during the periods in question will remember the extraordinary sexualization of occultism while Neptune was in Scorpio (1957–1970); the enthusiastic embrace of alternative realities once it moved into Sagittarius (1970–1984); the return to traditional occultism that followed Neptune's passage into Capricorn (1984–1998); and so on—and so did the ordinary vagaries that beset any phenomenon of the cultural fringes. Even so, by the time Pluto began its descent from planetary status in 2006 aspiring students of the occult had access to a banquet of classic texts and capably written manuals that their equivalents a few decades earlier could only dream of having. The longing for cosmos had become a potent force, and the cultural tides were clearly running its way.

The arts, always among the most sensitive barometers of the zeitgeist, also caught the changing currents of our time. One of the most intriguing artistic trends of the last decade or so of the twentieth century was the beginnings of a resurgence of classic forms and techniques in the fine arts. Over much of the Western world, painters and sculptors began to reject the modern and postmodern cult of ugliness and meaninglessness and returned to representational art that was beautiful and technically skilled. A network of independent schools, of which Jacob Collins's Grand Central Atelier in New York is among the most famous, has emerged in response, passing on traditional methods of art through the old and effective system of apprenticeship. So far the work of artists trained in these schools has been rigorously shut out by the iron triangle of mainstream art schools, art museums, and grant-making organizations that control the official art world. Media personality Morley Safer, a longtime fan of Jacob Collins and his school, explained that exclusion in terms that are harsh but not unfair: "The current art establishment, the so-called gatekeepers hate the kind of skill and craft and vision that an artist like Collins has."

The same revolt against the Plutonian cult of ugliness has also begun in the realm of art music, with musical prodigy Alma Deutscher among the leading rebels. Born in 2005 Deutscher began playing piano and violin at an age when most children are occupied with dolls and toy trucks and composed her first piano sonata at the age of five. Her opera *Cinderella* premiered in Vienna in 2016 to rave reviews and a standing ovation from the audience. Despite constant pressure from critics and the musical establishment to conform to current fashions and write ugly, discordant, meaningless music, Deutscher relies on the classical toolkit of tonality and harmony, producing impressively beautiful compositions. Her 2017 response to critics who insisted that beautiful music was outdated was typical, and lethal: "But I think that these people just got a little bit confused. If the world is so ugly, then what's the point of making it even uglier with ugly music?" In her wake other composers have begun to find their way back to music that reflects *cosmos,* the beautiful order of the pre- and post-Plutonian worlds.

Perhaps the most intriguing sign that an appreciation of cosmos was stirring as Pluto's influence waned, however, came from within modern science itself. In 1981 the biologist Rupert Sheldrake published *A New Science of Life,* in which he proposed that certain perplexing results of research into the life sciences could best be explained if growth and form in living matter is shaped by subtle patterns of beautiful order he named *morphogenetic fields.* His theory was predictably and savagely denounced by the scientific establishment—a furious editorial in the prestigious journal *Nature* described his book as "the best candidate for burning there has been for many years"—but Sheldrake continued his research, carrying out experiments to test his hypothesis and providing all the details so that readers could replicate the experiments and ponder the results. Over the last four decades Sheldrake has become one of the anchor points of a loose network of researchers and theoreticians exploring the world of meaningful connection and beautiful order that was ruled off limits by the scientific mainstream as the Plutonian age dawned.

So far, their work continues to be condemned harshly by right-thinking intellectuals and strictly excluded by the gatekeepers of the scientific professions. How long that exclusion will continue is an interesting question. On astrological grounds it seems likely that the remaining resistance to ideas such as Sheldrake's will crumble by 2036—and with it will go a worldview that by then will have outlived its time.

SEVEN

After Pluto

Back in 1962, around the time that the Plutonian era peaked and began its long decline, historian of science Thomas S. Kuhn published a book titled *The Structure of Scientific Revolutions.* He had become interested in the process by which the scientific community discards one set of theories about nature and takes up another and set out to explore how that had taken place over the years since modern science emerged in the seventeenth century. The conventional wisdom in his time held that this was a straightforward process in which old theories were discarded once the results of experiments disproved them and replaced by new theories that did a better job of explaining the data. What Kuhn found, however, was something considerably more complex, and much more relevant to the transformations of our time.

Looking back over the history of every branch of science, he found long periods in which a given set of theories remained unchallenged even though evidence contradicting them piled up. In what Kuhn called periods of "normal science," scientists treated established theories as sacrosanct and made only minor changes to them, tweaking the details or coming up with elaborate ad-hoc hypotheses to shoehorn experimental observations into the existing structure of theoretical models. Only when conflicting evidence reached critical mass, or when the results of an experiment proved completely impossible to explain from within the existing set of theories, were those theories finally discarded and replaced by a different set that did a better job of explaining the anomalies. Even after that happened established scientists in the field continued to cling to the old theories. Only as they retired or died, and a younger generation of scientists took their places, did the new theory become the basis for a renewed period of "normal science."

That, Kuhn showed, was how the Copernican Sun-centered view of the solar system took over from the Ptolemaic Earth-centered view; how Darwin's theory of natural selection took over from the theory that every variety of living thing had been independently created in 4004 BCE by God; and how many other important changes in scientific theory had taken place. While Kuhn didn't explore this, the same process can be seen at work in many other fields of human activity. To cite an example from popular culture, think of the way that classic rock-and-roll music emerged out of the background of popular music in the 1950s, flourished in the 1960s, and faded out in the 1970s. In the fifties it gave performers and listeners alike a musical language that spoke to them in a way other kinds of music couldn't match; in the sixties rock groups pushed the boundaries as far as they could; by the seventies all the things that classic rock could say had already been said, and a younger generation turned to other kinds of music that spoke to their experience of the world in a way that classic rock could not.

The same process is mapped out by the rise and fall of Pluto, the planet of opposition to cosmos. In the dawning decades of the Plutonian era, from 1900 to 1930, everything Plutonian was new, fresh, exciting, and the new planet allowed the generations that witnessed the First World War and its aftermath to make sense of their experience of the world in a way that the more familiar planetary influences did not. During Pluto's heyday, from 1930 to 2006, the Plutonian influence spread outward into every aspect of human life, fossilized into an orthodoxy, and began to crack as the anomalies piled up. In the waning decades of the Plutonian era, from 2006 to the present, that orthodoxy remains in place as an increasingly brittle shell and will doubtless continue to do so until sometime around 2036, when the shell will give way at last. Like the old scientists who cling to once-accepted theories, the institutions, social movements, and personalities that have benefited most from the Plutonian era can be expected to cling to their present positions until a rising generation—the generation born after 2006—reaches maturity and sets out to make its own mark on the collective conversation of our time.

ASTROLOGY AFTER PLUTO

That process will among other things have important effects on astrology itself. As the Plutonian era wanes, to begin with, the influence of Pluto itself will wane accordingly. That has already begun. If my experience with natal charts is anything to go by, the often-strident warnings of what people can expect when a transiting or progressed planet makes an aspect with Pluto's place in a natal chart are already somewhat outdated. I have repeatedly watched planets square or oppose natal Pluto by transit or progression and produce minor disturbances or none at all in the lives of the people thus affected. That seems to happen most consistently with people whose natal charts have Pluto weakly placed and with no important aspects to other planets. As we'll see shortly, this echoes other details of astrological experience, and helps us sketch out the role that the dwarf planet Pluto (and other bodies belonging to the same category) will play in the post-Plutonian era.

Another important shift that can be expected in post-Plutonian astrology is that the personality-centered astrology that has dominated the field since Pluto was discovered will become less central to astrological practice. As noted earlier, the interpretive techniques that astrologers developed once they started using horoscopes as keys to self-discovery rather than guides to destiny count as a significant addition to the toolkit of the working astrologer, and so there is no risk that they will be abandoned. Instead, it seems most likely that personality astrology will become a distinctive branch of the whole science of the stars—the kind of astrology that astrologers and clients use by choice when self-knowledge, rather than some other goal, is the point of their inquiries.

One likely core difference between Plutonian and post-Plutonian astrology will simply be that there will be other goals available to astrologers and their clients, and the exploration of personalities will no longer be the only game in town. The illusion of perfect freedom that was central to personality-centered, choice-centered astrology too often made it impossible for astrologers to offer meaningful answers to important questions: Why do all my relationships end up failing in the same way? Why did my business go under? Why can't I achieve my heart's desire no matter how hard I try? The techniques of classical natal astrology can answer these, and help clients understand where they face limits that they will have to live with and where different approaches will allow them to achieve what they want along unexpected routes. Those techniques and the guidance they permit will be at least as important to the working post-Plutonian astrologer as the methods that have been standard for the last three quarters of a century, while Pluto reigned.

Another significant difference between Plutonian and post-Plutonian astrology will likely be the resurgence of the branches of astrology that do not make use of natal charts and do not focus on the individual at all. Mundane astrology, the astrology of politics and nations, is among the prime candidates for revival, and certain tentative steps in this direction have already been taken in recent years. The era during which most astrologers tried to predict the fate of nations by using the natal charts to gauge the personalities of national leaders, because they knew of no other resource for the purpose, are already waning as more astrologers learn how to cast and delineate ingress charts and begin to pay attention to such longer-range techniques as the great conjunctions of Jupiter and Saturn and the precession of the equinoxes.

All these methods start from the recognition that the fates of nations are shaped by patterns far greater than the choices and personalities of individual human beings. In an era dominated by the opposition to cosmos, that recognition was all but unthinkable, but the descent of Pluto from planetary status is opening a door by which it can return.

Through that same door other branches of the astrological art such as horary astrology (astrological divination), electional astrology (the art of timing human actions by astrology), and medical astrology can find their way back into general use among astrologers.

Yet it is crucial to note here that Pluto has not been disproved like Vulcan, nor has it been reduced in status as far as Ceres was in the 1850s. The same decision of the International Astronomical Union that demoted Pluto from planetary status created a new category of dwarf planets to which Pluto and Ceres were both assigned. Like any other redefinition of the nearby heavens, this change represents a significant shift in our understanding of the solar system and thus, by the thesis explored in this book, marks a shift in the way that we, as a species, as nations and communities, and as individuals, relate to the complex influences that descend from the skies to affect all things on Earth.

The dwarf planets do not rank among the major principles of the heavens—that status is reserved for the planets—but they are set apart from the minor bodies, the asteroids, comets, and ordinary Kuiper Belt objects that provide the solar system with its small fry. They occupy an intermediate status, whose astrological role still awaits the patient analysis of horoscopes that will make its meaning clear. At present there are five confirmed dwarf planets in the solar system—Ceres, Pluto, Eris, Makemake, and Haumea—and at least five more Kuiper Belt objects that may turn out to be dwarf planets on further investigation. These represent one of the most fascinating fields for future astrological research. Two of them, Ceres and Pluto, are familiar to astrologers; the third, Eris, has been the focus of systematic study by astrologers since its discovery in 2005, and work has begun on the others. Decades of research will be needed to sort out their varied influences and get an overall sense of what role dwarf planets play in natal horoscopes and other astrological charts, but some of the work has already been done and much more of it is in process.

Some hints of the role of dwarf planets in post-Plutonian astrology can already be glimpsed by examining the way that the dwarf planet Ceres affects natal charts. As noted in chapter 3, the influence of Ceres has been worked out in some detail, following the lead of Demetra George's useful book *Asteroid Goddesses*. In my own astrological practice, I have found quite consistently that when Ceres is close to one of the angles of the chart—the ascendant, descendant, zenith, or nadir—or in a strong aspect to one of the planets, issues surrounding food and nurturing are unusually important to the person in whose chart it is.

The nature of the relationship the person has to these issues depends, as always, on the specifics of the chart. For example, one person whose natal chart I have studied has Ceres conjunct Venus close to the ascendant. She has very strong emotional responses to food, to the extent that she reads cookbooks for the sheer pleasure of imagining making and eating the dishes described in them. She also has a strong and insistent need to feel nurtured, especially but not only by means of food. Inquiry into her biography revealed that she had been starved by an abusive parent in early childhood and has had a complicated relationship with food ever after. By contrast, charts in which Ceres was neither angular nor in aspect to a planet have belonged just as consistently to individuals for whom food was of little emotional importance and whose life histories have been marked by no particular food-related issues.

This is only one astrologer's experience, of course, and many other voices will take part in the dialogue through which the astrological influence of Ceres as a dwarf planet will be settled. Once Pluto has completed its descent to dwarf planet status, however, it seems likely to me that it will have a comparable role in natal charts, especially for those people born after 2006. Those who have Pluto in one of the angles of their natal chart, or in an important aspect to one of the planets, will likely have Plutonian themes play important roles in their psychology and the course of their lives—potentially, if Pluto's position in the natal chart is strong enough, as influential as it was in most charts during Pluto's career as a planet.

Meanwhile, those whose natal charts assign no such importance to Pluto may not experience any of Pluto's influence at all, and astrologers will be able to anticipate by checking Pluto's position and aspects whether someone will face Plutonian upsurges from the subconscious mind, or not. Once the influences of the other dwarf planets have been worked out—a process that may take a very long time, since all the other Kuiper Belt objects move around the zodiac much more slowly than Pluto, and thus change signs over more than generational time scales—it seems likely that similar considerations will apply to them as well.

In these hints and fragments, we can begin to glimpse the first outlines of the mature post-Plutonian astrology that will emerge over the centuries ahead as the solar system's remaining dwarf planets are identified and their astrological influences sorted out. Pluto's connection to the zodiacal sign Scorpio seems to be well founded—certainly I have found in studying charts that Pluto in Scorpio behaves like a planet in the sign it rules—and there seems to be equal merit in seeing Ceres as the co-ruler of Virgo, as some astrologers have proposed. Which dwarf planets serve as co-rulers of other signs is a topic that can only be settled by much more work, and the exaltations and falls of the dwarf planets will also need to be worked out by careful study—to say nothing of minor dignities such as terms and faces, which are so important in horary astrology and some other branches of the astrological art.

The possibility that smaller bodies such as asteroids and Kuiper Belt objects will also turn out to have similar relationships with zodiacal signs deserves attention along the same lines. In medieval and Renaissance astrology, individual fixed stars were assigned planetary affinities, so the prospect of a greatly enriched concept of zodiacal relationships among objects in the heavens is not even particularly new. In an era marked by the rebirth of cosmos, such connections are likely to make more sense to astrologers than they did in the Plutonian era, when the concept of a beautifully ordered universe was in eclipse.

POST-PLUTONIAN PREDICTIONS

The changes we can expect in astrology, of course, are only one facet of the broader cascade of changes that can be anticipated as the last years of the Plutonian era give way to the opening years of the post-Plutonian era. As we have already seen, the descent of Ceres from planetary status saw the transformative cultural and political movement of romanticism fade out so completely that works of literature and art that shook audiences to the core in 1775 were forgotten a century later.

Consider the Ossian poems, a collection of verses penned by Scottish poet James McPherson in the late eighteenth century based on the Gaelic legends of Fionn mac Cumhaill. These poems had an immense cultural impact in their day. No less a figure than Napoleon Bonaparte was a passionate fan and kept a copy of the Ossian poems by his bedside all through the Napoleonic wars, and painters of the Romantic period filled countless canvases with scenes from McPherson's work. The Ossian poems, for that matter, are the reason you've heard of the man's name Oscar. McPherson used that name for one of the characters, and it caught on. Until you read these words, had you even heard of Ossian?

Not all the creations of the Romantic era vanished as completely as the poems of Ossian or Goethe's *The Sorrows of Young Werther*, to be sure. The Romantic music of Beethoven, Chopin, and the best of their contemporaries, for example, remained vital while most of the rest of Romantic culture sank into oblivion, and certain aspects of romantic nationalism became part of the ordinary language of national politics and retained that status long after Ceres had fallen from her former planetary status. The same thing happened to a lesser extent after Vulcan and Lilith had their brief periods of importance on the astrological stage.

What happens in the wake of a former planet's downgrading is a sorting process. In that process, certain things that reflected the temporary influence of the planet reorient themselves to other planetary energies, in much the way that occultism passed from the Moon to Mercury and then to Neptune, Lilithian witchcraft embraced the triumph of the Moon, and certain aspects of Cerean romantic nationalism were taken over by the Plutonian politics of communism and fascism. Meanwhile, the rest of the products of the temporary planet's influence lose popularity or drop into complete obscurity.

A comparable destiny lies in wait for the legacy of the Plutonian era over the years immediately ahead of us. As the influence of Pluto wanes, the social and cultural phenomena that influence inspired can be expected to wane with it, or to reorient themselves to echo the influence of some other planet. As already noted, many of these phenomena have already tracked the decline in Pluto's apparent size and importance with a remarkable degree of precision, and they can be expected to finish that course by the time Pluto finishes the approximately thirty-year period of twilight it began in 2006. Some will fade into complete obscurity, while others will redefine themselves as other planetary influences take over Pluto's former role. Here are some of the consequences I expect to see.

Nuclear Fission

The splitting of the atom, as we have seen, was arguably the most quintessentially Plutonian event in modern history. As the Plutonian influence rose to its zenith, nuclear fission accordingly provided the era with its most widely used anchor both for its dreams of limitless abundance and power, and for its nightmares of sudden obliteration and mass death. As the Plutonian influence waned, in turn, it provided one of that era's most widely used anchors for overblown hype and promises that would never be fulfilled, the keynote of Pluto's twilight years.

Of all the many practical applications of fission technology, nuclear power takes the lead in this process. As I write these words, for example, the nuclear industry and its publicists are making yet another attempt to market fission power to the general public as clean, safe, natural, and renewable. They are unlikely to get any further with this push than they have with the last half dozen or so, because the adjective that matters—affordable—is the one that nuclear power has never been able to achieve and will never be able to achieve. More than three-quarters of a century of experience has shown that nuclear power plants can only break even with the help of huge and continuing government subsidies. As the Plutonian era trickles away, the willingness of governments and ratepayers alike to keep a collection of nuclear white elephants trudging along, producing electrical power at a loss, is unlikely to last long.

By 2036, therefore, I expect the last commercial nuclear power plants anywhere to be scheduled for permanent shutdown if they have not already gone offline forever. Some smaller reactors will doubtless stay in operation to produce radioactive materials for medicine and raw materials for nuclear weapons, at least for a while. The thousands of tons of spent fuel rods and other high-level nuclear waste left over from the failed experiment of nuclear power, which will keep on emitting lethal doses of radioactivity for around a quarter of a million years, will be one of the most enduring legacies of the Plutonian era, and figuring out how to store that legacy safely will be an ongoing problem for our descendants for many millennia to come.

Given Pluto's deep connection with the symbolism of death, it is doubtless no accident that the military applications of nuclear power turned out to be much more useful than the civilian side of the equation. The nuclear-powered carriers and submarines of the Cold War era are nonetheless nearly obsolete. In an age of hypersonic cruise missiles, aircraft carriers are hopelessly vulnerable, and recent generations of diesel-electric submarines are just as stealthy as their nuclear equivalents and much less expensive to build and operate. I expect both, along with other nuclear-powered naval vessels, to be retired from active service by 2036.

Nuclear weapons are another matter. The coming of age of the atomic bomb in 1945 put a sudden stop to the cataclysmic global wars of the early twentieth century, because strategists on all sides discovered that there is no way to win a nuclear war. The absence of global wars since 1945 should therefore be considered Pluto's greatest gift to the world. I expect every major power, and some regional powers such as France and Israel, to maintain nuclear arsenals past the end of the Plutonian era, as a final guarantee of national survival and a means to keep the world wars of the early twentieth century from recurring.

That said, both the United States and the Russian Federation have vastly more nuclear weapons than are needed for the task of deterrence, and nuclear weapons are extremely expensive to maintain—uranium and plutonium are both very soft metals, so soft that their own weight causes them to slump over time, and the excruciatingly fine tolerances needed for nuclear weapons require warhead components to be machined back into spec every year or so. As the Plutonian era wanes, it will be easier for policymakers to measure the costs of nuclear weapon maintenance against the benefits of deterrence. I thus expect a treaty reducing both nations' nuclear arsenals to a few hundred warheads each to be negotiated by 2036 at the latest.

Space Travel

There is perhaps no greater mismatch between Plutonian fantasy and terrestrial reality than the gap between what the Space Age was supposed to bring us and what it actually provided. As noted back in chapter 6, the grandiose dream of interplanetary colonization and settlement fostered by science fiction ground to a sudden halt in the 1970s as space probes demonstrated that outside the protection of the Earth's magnetosphere, the solar system is full of hard radiation inimical to human life. For almost half a century now, as a result, popular culture has remained fixated on a vision of the future that will never happen. As the Plutonian era ends, that unwelcome reality will sink in.

Since the dream of space travel is so emotionally important to so many people, and so deeply interwoven with fantasies of exploration and discovery that date from centuries before Pluto's time, it will not sink in at once. I confidently expect at least two more sets of human bootprints to mark the Moon's gray face before the Plutonian era ends—the People's Republic of China has proposed this as a goal for its capable and (so far) successful space program; the United States has recently declared that it will be returning to the Moon within the present decade, and I see no reason to doubt that both nations will make good on their promises. Like the Apollo missions, however, these missions will mark the end of an era, not the beginning of one. Once these landings have allowed China to announce its status as a rising world power, and the United States to try to deny its status as a world power in decline, both nations will find other things to do with their respective resources and technical expertise.

Earth satellites, which are governed by Mercury rather than Pluto, will remain a viable technology thereafter, at least for a while. Most Earth orbits are so crowded at this point that scientists for some decades now have discussed worriedly the prospect of a "Kessler syndrome"—a chain reaction in which one collision between satellites sends fragments spalling off at orbital speeds to hit other satellites, until an entire region of space is so full of flying shrapnel that no satellite can survive there until Earth's gravity drags the debris down to burn up in the atmosphere. In low Earth orbits such as the one where the International Space Station circles, that clearing process will take decades; in mid-range orbits it will take centuries or millennia; in the high orbits where geosynchronous satellites circle, it will take longer than our species is likely to survive.

Whether a Kessler-syndrome disaster is likely to happen in the near future is a point hotly debated by scientists, and whether any workable technological solution would remedy such a disaster is another. It's hard to think of any end to the Space Age more perfectly in keeping with the symbolism of Pluto, but as the Plutonian era wanes, that symbolism and the influences that it represents are waning as well. The survival of satellite technology thus remains one of the great unknowns of the post-Plutonian future.

Communism

As we saw in chapter 2 and chapter 5, Marxism began its historical career under the influence of Neptune, one of an assortment of radical systems of political economy that rose to prominence in fringe culture in the second half of the nineteenth century. Most of the others vanished without a trace as Marxism morphed into Marxist-Leninist communism under the influence of Pluto, and the world split asunder in the best Plutonian style. While the Cold War held the planet in its grip, there was no room for a third alternative, much less the gallimaufry of radical political theories that makes the second half of the nineteenth century such a fascinating field for the historian of forgotten ideologies.

The Cold War turned out to be far more fragile than even the optimists of the time expected, however. Communism in Russia and Eastern Europe imploded messily even before the era of Pluto was over, while nations such as China that retained it in theory quietly shelved it in practice, permitting private ownership of industries again. Even before that change hit, beginning in the late 1960s, Marxist parties outside the Soviet sphere slipped back into Neptune's sphere of influence—that is to say, they stopped acting like the fearsomely disciplined revolutionary cadres of Lenin's day, and started acting like the would-be revolutionaries of 1848.

Like their nineteenth-century equivalents, the New Left in the United States and western Europe thus spawned factions such as the Weather Underground, the Symbionese Liberation Army, and the Baader-Meinhof Gang, which each committed a certain number of terrorist actions, and then were crushed by the police. Later Marxist outbursts in the United States, such as the Antifa movement that seized so many headlines and accomplished so little else in 2020, followed exactly the same course. It was all very reminiscent of the scene from Thomas Mann's novel *Buddenbrooks* cited in chapter 2: "Outbursts of passionate emotions and loudly chanted slogans, without any of the necessary clarity of intention or grasp of strategy needed in order to become a significant force for change."

Since there seems to be no reason to think that Neptune will ever be downgraded from planetary status, I expect that pattern to continue after 2036. Marxism is unlikely to maintain its Plutonian role as the standard by which all other radical movements were measured, though it is an interesting question whether the Neptunian radical ideologies of the post-Plutonian era will resemble those of the pre-Plutonian world, or whether they will veer off in new directions. Meanwhile, Uranian revolutions have already made a considerable comeback in recent decades, with capably executed popular uprisings and struggles for independence taking place in Africa and various parts of post-Soviet Eurasia. Since Uranus is also apparently here to stay as a planet, revolutions under its influence will likely be an important fact of political life into the far future.

Psychoanalysis

The splitting of the personality, as we've seen, was as essential a part of Plutonian culture as the splitting of the atom, and the history of psychoanalysis paralleled the history of nuclear power in its descent from great expectations to general irrelevance. Here, as with communism, much of that trajectory has already completed itself. Freud's reputation is already in tatters as biographers dig through the less savory parts of his life, casting an unsparing light on his enthusiasm for cocaine as a cure-all (and his consequent addiction), his attitudes toward women and female sexuality, and his dubiously ethical behavior toward some of his patients. His theories have come in for equally unfavorable assessment by writers who have pointed out that many of them are demonstrably false and much of the structure of Freudian psychoanalysis rests on arbitrary interpretations and untestable assumptions. Meanwhile, the system of therapy he founded has fallen into widespread disfavor and, increasingly, into disuse as well.

Over the years ahead, as Pluto finishes its descent from planetary status, that process will continue, and Freud's theories will follow their current trajectory toward the fringes. By 2036, accordingly, I expect Freudian psychoanalysis to have dropped out of use throughout the psychiatric mainstream. At best, it may find a niche market among those consumers of alternative healing modalities who still make use of such once-popular systems as reflexology and macrobiotics; at worst, it may suffer the same fate as phrenology—another system of personality analysis created by an iconoclastic European physician, which had an impressive vogue in nineteenth-century Europe and America. It claimed to read personal characteristics from bumps on the skull. Now and again antique shops in older American cities turn up porcelain model heads once used to train phrenologists, with the different regions of the head marked with their supposed meanings. It seems likely that copies of Freud's collected works may be found in the used bookstores of the 2060s in much the same way, as battered legacies of a forgotten art.

One offshoot of the psychoanalytic movement that may experience a different fate is the school created by Freud's student and rival Carl Jung. As a method of psychotherapy, Jungian analytical psychology has all the same issues and limitations as Freudian psychoanalysis, and Jung's biography and ideas have attracted much the same critical attention as Freud's. Unlike Freud's system, however, Jung's writings and ideas attracted attention early on in various corners of the alternative spirituality scene, and they have retained a presence there, especially among occultists, even as Jungian therapy has lost ground in psychiatric circles.

At this point, as a result, there is every reason to think that Jung's thought may end up finding a new home among occultists and spiritual dissidents, either as an important influence on future systems or as a complete system in its own right. Jungian practices such as active imagination already have close equivalents in modern Western alternative spirituality, and many of the relevant concepts match up just as well. The differences between the Self in Jung's writings and the Higher Self in occult literature, for example, or between Jung's concept of individuation and the concept of enlightenment in today's alternative spirituality, are minimal at best. None of this is accidental. Jung had a lifelong fascination with occultism; his doctoral dissertation was on the psychology of occult phenomena, his famous (and until recently secret) *Red Book* is full of occult symbolism, and he is known to have used his patients' horoscopes as a guide to therapy. It therefore makes an ironic kind of sense that his system of thought should end up being absorbed by the alternative spiritual tradition that inspired so much of it.

Yet there is of course an astrological dimension to this process as well. The descent of Pluto from its former planetary status leaves the psychoanalytical movement without a home among the planets. With its focus on *Memories, Dreams, Reflections*—to borrow and repurpose the title of Jung's fascinating and evasive spiritual autobiography— Jungian psychology is well suited to find a new planetary patron in Neptune, and to continue into the post-Plutonian era under that new influence. Freud's own system, and those of most of the other psycho-analysts who were taught or inspired by him, are too deeply linked with the Plutonian influence to be likely to have any significant future role once Pluto finishes its twilight.

Modern Art

The deliberate pursuit of ugliness and meaninglessness in art, music, and architecture is, as we have seen, another of the most distinctive expressions of the Plutonian influence in our time. While nuclear power stumbled from one financial disaster to another, manned space travel huddled beneath the safety blanket of Earth's magnetosphere from the early 1970s on, communist regimes imploded or quietly embraced capi-talism, and Freudian psychoanalysis lost the cultural cachet it once had and slid down a well-greased slope toward oblivion, the Plutonian tra-dition in the arts remains bolted firmly in place. It is held there by the iron triangle of universities, funding sources, and venues for display or performance, all of which go out of their way to exclude works that fail to conform to the fossilized Plutonian standards of the recent past.

Fortunately, this is a familiar condition in the history of the arts. Every so often a rigid academicism settles into place in some part of the artistic world, exercising strict control over what can be shown or performed or built, and the result is a period of stagnation, repetition, and meaningless variations on an impoverished set of themes, like the one that afflicts the arts today. Examples include the reign of *opera seria* in European opera in the eighteenth century and the dominance of academic art in the second half of the nineteenth. In these and other cases, the barricades finally fell when a new generation of artists, composers, or architects rejected the fossilized conformity demanded by their elders, did something more interesting outside the officially accepted venues, and drew so large a share of the audiences and patrons away from those venues that the latter collapsed for lack of support.

One consistent feature of these transformative periods in the history of the arts is that once they have happened, most of the products of the once-dominant academic style vanish completely from view. There have been a few attempts to revive *opera seria,* but none of them get far—the operas written during that era are just too dull. Similarly, most of the academic paintings of the mid-nineteenth century gather dust in third-rate museums, studied only by graduate students desperate for a dissertation topic, because nobody else anywhere finds them of interest. In the same way, it's a safe bet that after 2036, as tastes among art and music connoisseurs shift, the products of the Plutonian era's rigidly academic pursuit of ugliness and meaninglessness will suffer much the same fate.

It seems very likely that future historians of the arts will describe the era from 1930 to 2006 as one of the fallow periods that occur now and again in the history of human creativity, and the artists, musicians, and architects they will remember from the years between 2006 and 2036 will be those whose work display the first stirrings of a new attention to beauty, meaning, and classic form. Those of my readers who are interested in the arts and have money to spend might wish to keep this in mind. Wealthy Americans visiting France in the last quarter of the nineteenth century found it easy and inexpensive to buy world-class collections of works by Impressionists, Symbolists, and other artists rejected by the Salon de Paris, and the paintings and sculptures those Americans collected went on to become famous and dizzyingly expensive in the decades that followed. In exactly the same way, those who keep an eye out for the rising movements of post-Plutonian art may find themselves similarly rewarded.

Plutonian architecture, finally, will encounter the same fate in a slightly different manner. Buildings ironically tend to be much more transitory than paintings or musical scores, since they have to receive constant maintenance to keep them from crumbling under the wear and tear of everyday use, and even the most famous products of celebrity architects routinely face demolition if they fail to serve their function well. Look up sometime how many of the commercial buildings designed by Frank Lloyd Wright, that profoundly Plutonian figure have been demolished since his time. It's a remarkably long list. A great deal of early Plutonian-era architecture has already been subjected to the unanswerable critiques of the wrecking ball, and I expect a great deal of the more recent excrescences of modern architecture to face the same fate as the revulsion against ugly, dysfunctional buildings becomes a significant social force. By 2075 or so, it seems likely that the last few surviving products of the International Style (or its later and even less coherent offshoots) will be the subject of historic-preservation campaigns. "Yes, it's horribly ugly," I imagine the campaigners saying, "but it's historic, and there's nothing else left like it in the entire state."

More generally, making sense of the post-Plutonian future requires us to let go of some deeply rooted but unhelpful habits of thought. The most important of these is the fixation on the idea that the only possible futures our species can have are either continued progress along the lines already laid down by modern industrial culture, on the one hand, or a sudden plunge into apocalyptic mass death on the other. It will come as no surprise to my readers that this fixation began to seize the imagination of the modern world in the first years of the twentieth century, or that it did not begin to lose its grip until after the turn of the millennium. After all, both sides of the apparent dichotomy are utterly Plutonian. What is progress as ordinarily conceived, after all, but an endless linear flight beyond all imaginable limits, separating us forever from the things that have defined all human existence up to this point? What is the end of the world so vividly foreseen by today's popular imagination, for that matter, but an irreparable break in the course of history, dividing all of time into before and after?

Those Plutonian fantasies remain very deeply rooted in contemporary popular culture, and it can take a serious effort of the imagination to get past them. I encourage readers to make that effort, however, in order to get past the simplistic notions of a fading era and gain a broader glimpse of what the world of the post-Plutonian future can be: a world in which the rigid trajectory of progress-as-usual has given way to a less narrow sense of what the future can hold, and in which apocalyptic daydreams have been handed back to the religious traditions that spawned them. Try to imagine a landscape of the future defined neither by the straight line of progress nor the sudden stop of apocalypse, but by cycles—the same cycles, in fact, that astrologers have been tracking for the last five millennia and more. Imagine a future in which cultures and civilizations rise and set, new arts and sciences are born and old ones die out, and nations and peoples not yet born will have their hour on the stage. Eventually the era when Uranus and Neptune were newly discovered worlds, and Ceres and Pluto had their brief careers and planets, will be a distant era as far in the past as the discovery of the five visible planets is to us, and astrologers will study the surviving records of ancient European and American star lore to catch glimpses of their own distant roots.

All this may seem familiar to readers who know something about history, and it should. One of the most interesting things about the landscape of the future ahead of us, in fact, is that it will inevitably have important similarities to the landscapes of the past. This doesn't mean that the future will resemble any particular era of the past, of course. A Roman scholar in 21 CE, say, who spent his days reading the historical writings of Varro and Polybius, would have been wrong to think that the twenty centuries ahead of him would copy the details of the twenty centuries before his time. Even so, the rise and fall of cities and nations and cultures, the ebb and flow of populations, the processes by which artistic and intellectual movements budded and blossomed and went to seed, turned out to follow patterns he would have recognized at once.

There are, of course, two important differences between the future our imaginary Roman might have tried to foresee and the future we are facing. Those differences are neatly summed up by two planets, Uranus and Neptune, which played no known role in the Roman sky, or in any era afterward until the dawn of the modern age but will play inescapable parts in the post-Plutonian future. The concept of individual rights and the collective responsibility of society for its most vulnerable members, the political keynotes of Uranus and Neptune respectively, will be significant factors in the societies of the future. So will scientific discovery, another central theme of Uranus, and the exploration of alternative lifestyles and social forms, another central theme of Neptune. These and other expressions of the Uranian and Neptunian currents, however, will find places for themselves in a matrix of astrological forces in which the seven traditional planets continue to exert their usual influences.

Thus, the future ahead of us will not duplicate our past, but it will follow some of the patterns that can be traced in our past. The technologies will be different, to be sure, but then Rome's technologies were not the same as ancient Egypt's, just as ancient Egypt's were different from those of the first cities of the Neolithic Revolution—and just as the technologies of cultures yet unborn will differ from ours, in ways we can't possibly imagine. Some may be more complex than ours, some may be less, but all of them will be shaped by the needs and desires and interests of people who see the world in their own ways, not in ours.

The post-Plutonian future, in other words, is a very large place, with ample room for civilizations, cultures, and subcultures we cannot imagine, guided by ideals we have not yet conceived and shaped by experiences we have not yet encountered. Ironically, that future is far broader than the futures posited by most recent science fiction in every sense but a purely spatial one. So many current visions of the future simply project current political, economic, social, cultural, and artistic fashions onto a scale of light-years that it can be challenging to remember that the future can be something other than a prolongation of the present with bigger, faster machines, on the one hand, or bigger body counts on the other.

That effort needs to be made as we move closer to the final stages of Pluto's twilight. In the era about to dawn before us, the rebirth of cosmos will be fact of the first importance, culturally, psychologically—and spiritually. It is to that last dimension of Pluto's message that we now turn.

EIGHT

The Cosmos Reborn

As the planet of opposition to cosmos, Pluto has had a profound influence on modern life and thought. Many of the unquestioned assumptions of our era rest squarely on the Plutonian rejection of the beautiful order of things, the concept of cosmos that was recognized and revered by the cultures and philosophies of the past. The abandonment of cosmos has all too often been treated as the touchstone of modernity, the factor that sets us apart from the humanity of the past and will remain in place into the indefinite future. That this abandonment may turn out to be temporary is quite simply unthinkable to a great many people in the present world.

We can measure the impact of that unthinkable but inescapable turn of events through one of its manifestations in the world of scholarship. In 1904, as the first foreshocks of the Plutonian era were making themselves felt, the pioneering sociologist Max Weber published an influential book titled *The Protestant Ethic and the Spirit of Capitalism.* That book covered a great deal of ground, but one of its central themes gave a useful name to the Plutonian rejection of cosmos. The phrase Weber used was *die Entzauberung der Welt,* "the disenchantment of the world." Weber argued that the coming of the modern world marked the point at which people stopped believing in magic, spirits, and all the other colorful beliefs of the premodern world. More, he argued that this experience of disenchantment was central to modernity, and however sad it was to say goodbye to a world of magic and wonder, he claimed, modern people had no other choice.

It was not until 2017 that someone brought up the obvious absurdity at the heart of this claim. Jason Josephson Storm's book *The Myth of Disenchantment: Magic, Modernity, and the Birth of the Human Sciences* pointed out cogently that at the very time Weber was writing his book, he knew people in the early twentieth-century German occult scene who were practicing magic, communing with spirits, casting and reading horoscopes, and otherwise spending their days in a world from which *enchantment* in Weber's own sense of the word had by no means departed. For that matter, those un-disenchanted individuals were far from unique. The years during which Weber labored on *The Protestant Ethic and the Spirit of Capitalism* were also the years during which large occult organizations such as the Theosophical Society and the Hermetic Order of the Golden Dawn flourished, publishing firms turned out occult literature at a pace not to be exceeded until the great alternative-realities boom of the 1970s, supposedly outdated systems of thought and practice such as astrology went from strength to strength, and popular traditions of occultism thrived throughout the industrial world.

What was going on in Weber's time, in other words, was a Plutonian schism of a familiar sort, dividing society into a respectable minority who claimed to have left behind the world of magic and spirits, and an unmentionable majority who continued to practice magic, commune with spirits, read their destinies in the stars, and ignore the official pronouncements about what the world was or was not still allowed to contain. This schism is of crucial importance to our theme because a world full of enchantment, of magic and spirits and subtle connections linking all things together is a world that participates in cosmos. Study any of the classic works of Western occult philosophy, from *On the Mysteries* by Iamblichus of Chalcis and *Three Books of Occult Philosophy* by Henry Cornelius Agrippa to *Doctrine and Ritual of High Magic* by Eliphas Lévi and *The Golden Dawn* by Israel Regardie, and it's impossible to miss the centrality of a beautifully ordered universe to the Western occult tradition.

The crowning irony of the Plutonian era, then, was that cosmos never actually went away. It simply became unfashionable for a while in those social circles that claimed intellectual respectability, just as beautiful order in the arts became unfashionable among the self-anointed leaders of the artistic, musical, and architectural avant-garde during Pluto's reign. While Bertrand Russell preened himself on his capacity to settle comfortably on a supposedly firm foundation of unyielding despair, plenty of other equally modern, educated, up-to-date people lived in a universe just as beautifully ordered and meaningful as the worlds of their ancestors.

Unfashionable as it was for a time, the worldview of traditional Western occultism has much to say to the prospects that are opening up before us as the Plutonian era ends, and this final chapter will attempt to discuss a little of what might be drawn from that source.

THE TREE OF LIFE

Perhaps the most useful guide to the post-Plutonian cosmos available just now, in point of fact, is the traditional Western occult diagram known as the Tree of Life, a structure of ten circles and twenty-two lines that is held to communicate the subtle structure of the universe and everything in it. It is a diagram of the process by which the universe comes into being, from primordial unity (the first sphere or station, Kether) to the world as we see it around us (the tenth sphere or station, Malkuth). It is also a diagram of the process by which the individual soul awakens to its cosmic potential, rising up from unreflective life in the ordinary world, Malkuth, to unity with the source of all things, Kether.

The Tree of Life has a long history. It originated among ancient Greek Pythagorean mystics and passed from them to the Gnostics, from the Gnostics to mystical traditions within Judaism, from those to the broader current of Western esoteric traditions beginning in the

Renaissance. Despite this, it was only after 1854, when Eliphas Lévi made it central to the occult teachings passed on in his bestselling book *Dogme et Rituel de la Haute Magie* (*Doctrine and Ritual of High Magic*) that it became familiar to a wider public.

The ten circles, spheres, or stations of the Tree have many correspondences, but among the most important of these is a set of astrological meanings. In the Renaissance version that Lévi used, the tenth and lowest sphere—Malkuth, the Kingdom—is assigned to the Earth, and the next seven spheres are assigned to the two luminaries and five then-known planets in order of their apparent speed when observed from Earth. The Moon, as the swiftest of the seven great powers, is closest to Earth in the ninth station, Yesod, and Saturn, the slowest, is furthest away in the third station, Binah. The two remaining stations beyond Saturn were assigned to the fixed stars, which were thought to form a sphere in ancient astronomy, and the hypothetical Primum Mobile, the sphere that sets all the others into motion.

It has been a long time since anyone has believed that the stars form a sphere around a motionless Earth or that another sphere farther out sets the whole cosmic structure into motion. Occultists tend to be highly conservative, however, and the idea of assigning the more recently discovered planets to the Tree of Life took time to find favor. When that idea was eventually tried out, it faced an immediate challenge, for the simple reason that there were too many planets. It's essential to the structure of the Tree of Life that there can be ten and only ten spheres, but Pluto required an eleventh if it was going to be fitted into the scheme. Various arrangements were tried to deal with the interloper, none of them particularly successful.

The demotion of Pluto from planetary status solved that problem neatly. If Uranus and Neptune are placed on the Tree of Life in the order of their apparent speeds as seen from Earth, just like all the planets below them, all ten spheres of the Tree of Life are assigned to an astrological planet, and the symbolism of each of the spheres both matches and extends that of the corresponding planet.

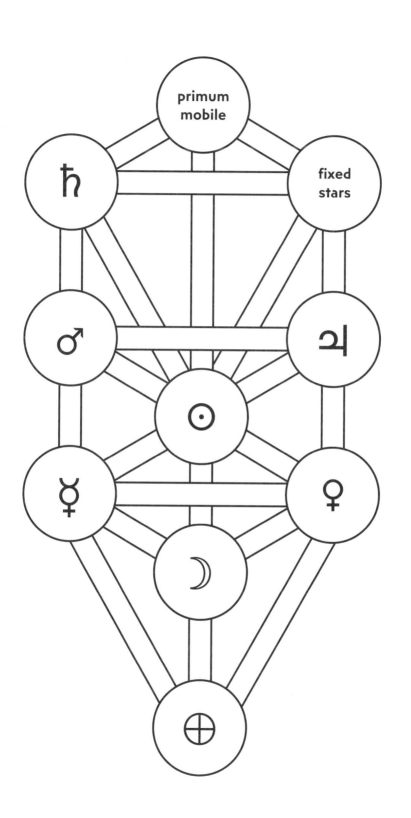

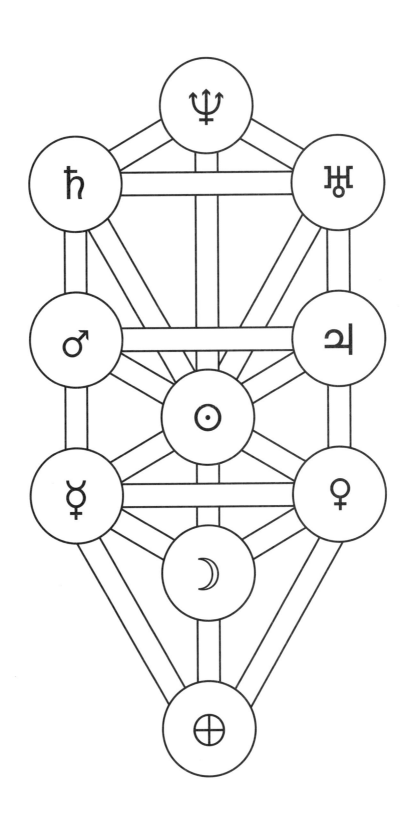

We can therefore begin making sense of the post-Plutonian cosmos by considering the ten stations of the Tree of Life one at a time, beginning from the top.

Kether—Neptune

Kether, the Crown, is the highest sphere on the Tree of Life, and it represents unity. It is strictly speaking incomprehensible to human consciousness, at least at our current stage of evolution. We can only understand something by contrasting it with something else, and at the level of being represented by Kether, there is no "something else"—all that exists is a single undifferentiated unity in which subject and object are merged. Thus, its reflections in our minds are always illusions and vague approximations. As the planet representing unity, Neptune partakes of this same character.

The highest and most positive expressions of the Neptune influence in human life accordingly take the form of mysticism, in which the individual seeks unity with God or the universe, and those spontaneous experiences of unity that psychologists tellingly call "oceanic." Further down the scale of human consciousness, it is reflected in the creative power of the human imagination; in occultism—which is the practical application of imagination in individual life—and in the alternative cultures of social and political radicalism, which are the practical applications of imagination in collective life. At the lowest level Neptune's influence expresses itself in alcoholism, drug abuse, and mental illness, the dissolution of the personality into an artificial or pathological unity with its surroundings.

Chokmah—Uranus

Chokmah, Wisdom, is the second sphere of the Tree of Life, and it represents the division of unity into duality. It represents dynamic energy, change, creative force, and the rupture of unity. Where Kether is often represented as a single point, Chokmah is a line extending to infinity. In Chokmah the possibility of an individual existence separate from the rest of the universe first begins to take shape, though this possibility does not complete its emergence until much lower on the Tree. As the planet representing individuality, Uranus expresses this same energy in all its manifestations in human life. It brings disruption and revolutionary change for good or ill. When its energies relate constructively to the rest of the horoscope, it brings originality, creative vision, and the courage to follow a uniquely personal path. When its energies conflict with the rest of the horoscope, it can lead to eccentricity, disruption, and isolation.

These first two planetary attributions require Neptune and Uranus to be assigned a depth of meaning and a symbolic importance they have not heretofore received, but which they arguably deserve. As the outermost planet in the solar system, Neptune is the Lord of the Great Deep, the astrological representative of infinity and eternity; as the planet of unity, Neptune stands in for the ground of being that philosophers have long identified with God. There is, however, something distinctly feminine about Neptune's influence, and I have come to think that the mythic astrology of civilizations of the far future will likely identify the blue planet at the solar system's outer edge, not with a sea-god, but with a sea-goddess, or perhaps a star-goddess such as the Egyptian deity Nut. Similarly, Uranus is the firstborn of the Infinite, Phanes or Protogonos, the Promethean power that disrupts the primal unity so that cosmos can come into being. Now that these two influences have constellated as planets, they can be expected to appear far more clearly and forcefully in the mythological and spiritual thought of the future.

Binah—Saturn

The third sphere of the Tree of Life is Binah, Understanding, which balances Chokmah. Where Chokmah is force, Binah is form; where Chokmah is disruption, Binah is stability; where Chokmah is freedom, Binah is restriction. Here we are in territory familiar to generations of astrologers, for Saturn has long been recognized as the planetary expression of the Binah principle. Where astrology before the dawn of the Uranian era saw Saturn as the complement and opposite of Jupiter, however, the structure of the Tree of Life points out that it is at least as much the complement and opposite of Uranus: the firm structure that keeps Uranian force from diffusing itself into ineffectuality, the established arrangement of things that gives the revolutionary energy of Uranus a thrust-block against which it can push.

Chesed—Jupiter

The fourth sphere of the Tree of Life, Chesed or Mercy, is the great center of expansion on the Tree, the creative union of force and form that leads to growth, maturation, and development. For obvious reasons it has been identified since ancient times with Jupiter, the planet of harmonious growth and abundance. It represents the unfolding of Uranian dynamism balanced and tempered by Saturnian stability and form.

Geburah—Mars

The fifth sphere of the Tree of Life, Geburah or Severity, balances Chesed's growth. If Chesed may be seen as a flourishing tree, Geburah is the pruning-hook that cuts away damaged branches and keeps growth from going outside due bounds. Since ancient times it has been associated with Mars. If Mars is seen as Jupiter's complement and opposite, rather than that of Venus, the troublesome Martian energy can be put to constructive purposes more easily. Furthermore, this pairing makes it easier to recognize that Martian virtues and vices are found as often in women as in men.

Tiphareth—Sun

The central sixth sphere of the Tree of Life, Tiphareth or Beauty, is the stage of the process of cosmic creation at which individual things come into existence, and the stage in the process of spiritual growth at which individual beings attain self-knowledge and receive their first contact with the source of all. It is the point of equilibrium between the influences of Chokmah and Binah, as well as between those of Chesed and Geburah, and it is the complement and opposite of Kether, the fully realized individual face to face with the primordial, undifferentiated unity. Since ancient times it has been associated with the Sun, the astrological factor most deeply linked with individual identity. In the astrology of earlier times, the Sun has understandably been paired with the Moon. As we'll see, that pairing remains relevant in the post-Plutonian cosmos, but the Sun and Neptune also form a complementary pair—the center of the solar system balanced against its outermost planet, the individual face to face with the cosmos as a whole.

Netzach—Venus

The seventh sphere of the Tree of Life, Netzach or Victory, is the realm of the emotions and of the arts, the creative force of Chokmah brought down the planes of being into material manifestation. Since ancient times it has been associated with Venus, the planet of the emotional life and of the feminine principle. It is balanced by Hod-Mercury.

Hod—Mercury

The eighth sphere, Hod or Glory, is the realm of the intellect and the sciences, which study the forms of Binah as they descend the planes of being into material manifestation. In the scheme outlined by the Tree of Life, these two are complements and opposites. One of the reflections of this complementarity can be seen in the way that gender polarities have shifted over the course of recent history. Men corresponding to the Mars archetype—the warrior, the conqueror, the pioneer—have become much less common in the last few centuries, and that archetype itself has become much less central to the masculine self-image, while the Mercury archetype—the entrepreneur, the communicator, the skilled technician—has become correspondingly more widespread and psychologically important. That shift is not yet complete, and the confusion and difficulty in gender relationships just now will likely resolve as the shift completes in the years ahead.

Yesod—Moon

As the influences of the Chokmah-Binah pair and the Chesed-Geburah pair descend into balance in Tiphareth, those of Netzach and Hod descend into balance in Yesod, the Foundation, which synthesizes all the higher spheres of the Tree of Life and projects them down into material manifestation in the tenth sphere. The Moon has the same role in astrology, gathering up the subtle forces of the other planets and modulating their influence on the Earth. The Moon is the planetary ruler of biology, of all those aspects of human existence that are generically human, anchored in the body and the unconscious, biological levels of the mind. It thus forms a polarity with the Sun, the archetype of individual consciousness. On the Tree of Life, the Sun as the unique individual thus mediates between Lunar humanity-in-the-mass and the undifferentiated spirit of Neptune. The Moon, however, also has a mediating role, uniting the Sun-Tiphareth influence with Malkuth-Earth.

Malkuth—Earth

The tenth and final sphere of the Tree of Life, Malkuth, the Kingdom, is the world of ordinary experience, the place of manifestation of all the forces of the nine higher spheres. In astrology this is of course the Earth, expressed in the twelve houses of the individual horoscope and summed up in the ascendant or rising sign. Malkuth receives the emanations of the other spheres through Yesod in exactly the same way that the Earth receives the influences of the other planets modulated through the Moon—and in exactly the same way, the world and individual consciousness interact through the mediating influence of the body and the automatic, biological aspects of the mind.

PRIMARIES, SECONDARIES, AND TERTIARIES

The patterns we have just traced on the Tree of Life can be explored in another way, using numerological patterns familiar from astrological tradition and ancient occult symbolism alike. The idea of a sevenfold planetary order seems to be very deeply rooted in the human psyche and can be found in spiritual traditions from around the world. As we saw back in Chapter 1, however, the expression of that order central to traditional astrology required the Sun and Moon to be shoehorned in among the five visible planets, where they don't really fit. One of the less recognized consequences of the last three centuries of astronomical discovery and astrological research is that this oddity of symbolism can now be redressed.

There are in fact, in today's solar system, seven astrological planets properly so called: Mercury, Venus, Mars, Jupiter, Saturn, Uranus, and Neptune, in order of apparent motion from fastest to slowest, as seen from Earth. Jupiter, the largest planet in the solar system, quite appropriately occupies the central place in the sequence. To one side of Jupiter stand the three inner planets, which have their strongest influence on the life of the individual. On the other side stand the three outer planets, which have their strongest influence on the life of society and other collective phenomena. Placed between them, Jupiter naturally has equal influence on both the individual and the collective.

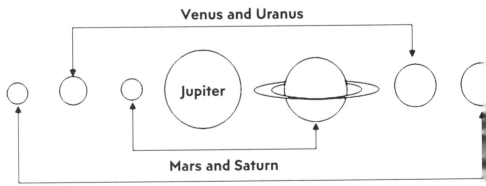

When arranged between the individual and the collective planets like this, furthermore, another set of complementary oppositions appears among the worlds to either side. Note how Mars contrasts with Saturn, the planet of change against the planet of stability, the irresistible force pitted against the immovable object. In the same way, Venus contrasts with Uranus, the planet of love and harmony, standing against the planet of disruption and personal uniqueness. Mercury, finally, has the same contrasting relationship with Neptune: reason against mysticism, the dividing and clarifying power of the Mercurial mind against Neptune's dissolution of all division into unity.

With the two luminaries no longer needed to fill gaps in the sevenfold sequence of planets, they can take on their proper dignity as two of the three primary influences on every horoscope. The third is, of course, the Earth, represented in astrological charts by the twelve house cusps and, above all, by the ascendant. The Sun, the Moon, and the rising sign are the primary indicators of personal identity in a natal horoscope and everything else in the chart is secondary to them. I can readily imagine astrologers of the future, in fact, dividing the influences at work in an astrological chart into the Three Primaries and the Seven Secondaries.

I encourage those of my readers who are astrologers, or who have learned enough about the art of astrology to know their way around a horoscope, to think about this subtly different way of understanding the influence of the heavens in an astrological chart. The Primaries, the Sun and Moon and ascendant, provide the basic frame within which all other influences have their places and extend a general influence over the entire chart that is shown by the signs and houses where they appear and their relationships with one another. The Secondaries, the seven planets properly so called, operate within that basic frame according to their own properties, the signs and houses in which they are placed, and the aspects they make with the Primaries and among themselves. In my experience, at least, this division between Primaries and Secondaries is a helpful tool for sorting out the complexities of an astrological chart and seems to make good delineations and accurate predictions a little easier.

And the Tertiaries? They certainly exist, and there is every reason to think that they will be recognized and taken into account by the astrologers of the future. Ceres and Pluto are two of them. The other three dwarf planets, Eris, Makemake, and Haumea, will likely turn out to belong to the same category, along with the largest asteroids and Chiron, the asteroid-sized mass of ice that orbits between Saturn and Uranus, which many recent astrologers have found useful in certain specialized applications. Research into the Tertiaries is still in its infancy. A great deal of work has been done on Pluto, though that will have to be adjusted to take into account the change in its status, and some work has been done on Ceres, Chiron, and some of the asteroids. The suggestions I offered in the previous chapter, based on my own experience with Ceres in natal charts, may be considered a tentative contribution to that work.

It can be tempting to imagine the directions in which astrology could develop in the post-Plutonian era as these changes settle into place. The sevenfold sequence formed by the five planets and two luminaries, for example, has a range of applications in astrological practice, extending from the planetary hours, through the annual planetary cycles originally published by Edgar de Valcourt-Vermont in 1901 and adopted by many astrologers since his time, to the immense historical vistas explored by Renaissance astrologer Johannes Trithemius in his essay *De Septem Secundeis* (*On the Seven Secondaries*). The possibility that the time-honored sequence including Sun and Moon might eventually be replaced by one based on the seven Secondaries, with Uranus in place of the Sun and Neptune in place of the Moon, is at least worth exploring. At some point in the far future, will ordinary calendars come to include Uransday and Neptunsday in place of Sunday and Monday?

Such speculations are entertaining, but the future will go its own way and astrology gives only the general outlines of the route it will take. In a very real sense, we are in the same situation as the astrologers of the first civilizations to recognize that Mercury, Venus, Mars, Jupiter, and Saturn were not merely five bright stars among millions but distinct powers of the heavens with their own influences on human life. While the influences of the planets Uranus and Neptune, the dwarf planets Ceres and Pluto, and a few asteroids have been sketched out by astrologers, a great deal of work remains to be done to refine and expand what is already known, and to figure out how these new influences relate to the whole art of astrology. Meanwhile the three newly discovered dwarf planets, Eris, Makemake, and Haumea, still await systematic astrological study, and so do plenty of other Kuiper Belt objects which may or may not turn out to be dwarf planets once enough is known about them. The next millennium or so, as a result, promises to be a very busy time for astrologers.

THE INITIATION OF THE NADIR

There's a definite temptation to think of the trajectory of Pluto, from its dawning as the elusive Planet X through its glory days as America's favorite planet to its long twilight of overblown hype and unfulfilled promises, as the chronicle of a mistake: we thought it was a planet, but then it turned out that it wasn't. Easy as this is, for reasons already covered at some length in this book, I'm convinced that it's misleading. As we've seen, the discovery of a new planet can be traced in history before the planet itself appears, and even those "planets" that turned out not to exist at all had a significant presence in human consciousness during the period when they were believed to exist.

Take the underlying philosophy of astrology as seriously as it deserves to be taken, and things appear in a different light. From this standpoint, Pluto was discovered when it was time for a rising influence in collective consciousness to find a suitable planetary anchor; its relentless shrinking over the decades that followed its discovery measured the waning of that influence, and the International Astronomical Union was moved by the stars in their courses to demote Pluto from planetary status when it was time for that influence to sink into the background of cosmic forces. The question that comes first to mind in this context is why that influence needed to be brought into focus at that time in human history.

Intriguingly, occult philosophy offers a potential answer. From ancient times the path of human existence has been understood by mystics and mages as a descent into matter, followed by an ascent back into spirit. Individual souls, those collective souls that we call cultures, and that great oversoul that is humanity as a whole, descend into material embodiment to learn the lessons that only the world of matter can teach, and having mastered those lessons, reascend to their original home, transformed and empowered by the experiences they have encountered on their journey. That narrative of human origin and destiny can be found explicitly in the *Corpus Hermeticum,* the collection of Greek mystical writings from Egypt that has been central to the Western occult tradition for many centuries. It can be found in countless other texts, ancient as well as modern, and it is also expressed in symbolic form in all those myths in which a divine or human protagonist descends into the underworld to accomplish some task and then ascends once more into the light of day.

The experience symbolized by those myths, and described in various ways in occult and mystical literature from around the world, seems to be a consistent factor in human spiritual development. At a certain point in the process of awakening, the seeker loses contact with everything outside the purely material dimensions of existence and must struggle on for a time without any response from the spiritual realms. The great Christian mystic Saint John of the Cross gave that experience a memorable name in the title of his most famous book *The Dark Night of the Soul.* Other mystical writings speak of it as a period of spiritual dryness or purgation. In occult literature, however, it has a name that refers back to the narrative of descent and return discussed above: the Initiation of the Nadir.

In astrology the nadir or *imum coeli* ("lowest part of heaven") is the cusp of the fourth house of an astrological chart, the lowest point on the ecliptic as seen from the place and time for which the chart is cast. In occult teaching it has another meaning—it is the lowest point in the soul's descent into matter, the point at which descent gives way to stillness and then to the journey of return. It is an inescapable part of the soul's journey. The twentieth-century occultist Dion Fortune compared it to the marker buoy in a yacht race, which every boat must reach and round before they put about and set course for home. Each soul passes through the material plane in exactly the same way, because only in the world of dense matter can the soul finish the process of awakening into full objective consciousness so that it can begin the long journey back to its spiritual source.

That pattern can be traced in the collective lives of human cultures just as clearly as in the lives of individuals. It's noteworthy in this context that every literate human society whose intellectual history is well-enough documented can be shown to have had its own age of reason—a stage of its history in which its intellectual elite abandoned traditional religious ideas for a time, embraced some form of rational philosophy in their place, and then later on turned back to spirituality and worked out a creative fusion of reason and religion.

The products of those ages of reason differ because cultures differ. The ancient Egyptian age of reason gave rise to the solar cult of Akhenaten; the ancient Chinese, to the ethical philosophy of Confucius; the Indian, to the mystical traditions of Buddhism and Jainism; the classical Greek and Roman, to the philosophy of Plato and Aristotle and the mathematics of Euclid; and the West, to experimental science.

Each of these cultures thus passed through a period in which its traditional vision of cosmos fell away. In each case, the age of reason gave rise to great intellectual and cultural innovations, and in every case but the present one, those were then woven back into the fabric of cosmos as the culture regained its vision of the beautiful order of things, renewed and enriched by the creative efforts of the age of reason. Ours has not yet taken this latter step, but our age of reason is still in process, and the last stages of its history are yet to be written. In the process of historical transformation that all other high cultures have undergone, and that ours will doubtless undergo in its time, we can see the workings of the Initiation of the Nadir in the lives of entire cultures.

Can we take the same insight one step further, and trace the process of descent and return in the life of humanity as a whole? I think we can. In our time, the human population has risen to its all-time high, and demographers are already discussing the first signs of the inevitable decrease in global population that will follow our era and return the world's population to a level that the planet can sustain indefinitely. From a mystical standpoint more human souls are in material incarnation in our time than ever before—and it seems very likely, given the ecological consequences of the current era of overpopulation, that there will never be so many human souls in incarnation again.

In our time, as a result, billions of people have experienced the world through Pluto's eyes, as a place without order and beauty—without cosmos. Is it too much to suggest that this marks the nadir of the long descent into matter that so many mystics and philosophers have discussed, not just for individuals or individual cultures, but for our species as a whole?

If this is in fact the inner significance of our time in the great trajectory of human history, Pluto's time as a planet was anything but a mistake. Instead, Pluto played a central role in one of the most critical transformations in the long history of our species. It took us millions of years here on Earth to reach the Initiation of the Nadir as a species, and it will doubtless take us millions more to finish our course even on this one plane of being. Still, it was during the era now closing around us—during the Plutonian era, the era from 1900 to 2036 when cosmos was in eclipse—that our species finished its descent into matter and began the slow path of ascent. It seems likely that in the far future, when our distant descendants look back on our time from inscrutable heights, they will have reason to be grateful to the little frozen world in the Kuiper Belt that rose briefly but powerfully to planetary status, so that it could help shepherd our species through the greatest transformation of all.

Glossary

ANGLES OF THE CHART: the ascendant, descendant, zenith, and nadir, the four strongest positions in an astrological chart.

ASPECT: one of a set of angles between two planets, as seen from Earth, which combine the influences of the planets in predictable ways.

ASTEROID: a small rocky body orbiting the Sun, so small that its gravity has not contracted it into a sphere. Most asteroids are in a belt between the orbits of Mars and Jupiter.

ASTRAEA: the fifth asteroid to be discovered.

CEREAN ERA: the period from 1771 to roughly 1880 when the asteroid Ceres functioned astrologically as a planet.

CERES: a dwarf planet in the asteroid belt, discovered in 1801 and originally mistaken for a planet.

CHARON: the largest of Pluto's moons.

CHIRON: a minor body orbiting the Sun between the orbits of Saturn and Uranus, studied by some modern astrologers.

CONSTELLATION: an arbitrary group of stars as seen from Earth, of no importance in modern astrology.

COSMOS: a Greek word meaning "beautiful order."

DWARF PLANET: a celestial body in this or another solar system that orbits a star rather than some other body and is massive enough that its gravity forms it into a spherical shape but not massive enough that its gravity clears the region through which it orbits of other stray bodies. Ceres, Eris, Haumea, Makemake, and Pluto are the five known dwarf planets in our solar system at present.

ECLIPTIC: the narrow belt of the sky through which the Sun, Moon, and planets move when observed from Earth.

ERIS: a dwarf planet located in the Kuiper Belt.

HAUMEA: a dwarf planet located in the Kuiper Belt.

HOUSE: one of twelve divisions of the sky, as seen from the location on Earth for which an astrological chart is cast; each house relates to certain aspects of human life.

JUNO: the third asteroid to be discovered, studied by some astrologers.

KUIPER BELT: a zone in the outer reaches of the solar system in which many small icy bodies are located.

LILITH: a hypothetical second moon of Earth whose existence was announced in 1898; never accepted by astronomers, it has been studied ever since by a few astrologers, and has also been redefined as one of several alternative points in the heavens.

LILITHIAN ERA: the period from 1868 to the present when some form of Lilith seems to have functioned astrologically in certain ways as a planet.

MAKEMAKE: a dwarf planet in the Kuiper Belt.

MANSIONS, LUNAR: twenty-eight roughly equal sections of the ecliptic, forming a lunar zodiac of importance in traditional Arabic and Indian astrology.

MUNDANE ASTROLOGY: the branch of astrology that deals with nations and politics.

NATAL ASTROLOGY: the branch of astrology that deals with the birth charts of individuals.

PALLAS: the second asteroid to be discovered, studied by some astrologers.

PLUTO: the closest of the Kuiper Belt bodies to the Sun, discovered in 1930 and originally mistaken for a planet, now classified as a dwarf planet.

PLUTONIAN ERA: the period from 1900 to 2036 when the Kuiper Belt body Pluto functioned astrologically as a planet.

PRECESSION OF THE EQUINOXES: a slow wobble in the Earth's axis of rotation that causes the equinox and solstice points to creep backward through the zodiac at a rate of one degree every seventy-two years.

PROGRESSION: technically known as "secondary direction," a method of predicting the course of a human life from the birth chart by advancing the chart one day to represent each year of the person's life; aspects made by progressed planets to planetary positions in the natal chart mark significant changes in the life of the person whose chart is being progressed.

QUAOAR: a Kuiper Belt body.

ROMANTICISM: an artistic, cultural, and political movement active between the 1770s and the 1880s, linked astrologically with the Cerean era.

SEDNA: a Kuiper Belt body.

SIGN: one of twelve 30° segments of the ecliptic, counting from the point where the Sun is located at the moment of the spring equinox. The signs are not the same as the constellations for which they were originally named.

TRANSIT: the movement of a planet in the heavens through an aspect with the position a planet had in a horoscope drawn up for an earlier time, such as a birth chart; planetary transits across birth chart positions mark significant changes in the life of the person whose chart is involved.

VESTA: the fourth asteroid to be discovered, studied by some astrologers.

VULCAN: a hypothetical planet predicted by Urbain Le Verrier in 1859, and studied by some astrologers. Its existence was finally disproved by Albert Einstein in 1915.

VULCANIAN ERA: the period from 1829 to 1945 when the hypothetical planet Vulcan functioned astrologically as a planet.

ZODIAC: the circle formed by the twelve astrological signs.

Notes

General information on a great many topics covered in this book can be found in any convenient reference source, such as Wikipedia. In particular, I have used Wikipedia as a convenient reference for the historical events mentioned in the pages above, so as to place my historical analysis on the basis of the current consensus among historians, and readers who want to know more about any of the events described here can begin their researches there.

INTRODUCTION

The demotion of Pluto is well described in Brown 2010, pp. 204–30, and the remarkable era of planetary discovery leading up to that demotion is covered in Brown 2010 more generally. The public reaction is covered in Brown 2010 and Tyson 2009. The astrological implications of a planet's discovery are discussed in Tarnas 2006, p. 95.

CHAPTER ONE.
THE ANCIENT HEAVENS

The science of archaeoastronomy—the study of the astronomical knowledge of ancient human societies—has expanded dramatically over the last half century or so; see, for example, Aveni 1989,

Cornell 1981, Krupp 1983, and North 2008. There are many good books on Stonehenge; I have relied especially on Souden 1997. Hawkins and White 1965 should be read by anyone interested in the monument. See Heggie 1981 for a more general summary of megalithic astronomy. For Hesiod, Wender 1973 is a readable translation. For the mansions of the Moon, Warnock 2006 is the one useful book in English; the first mansion, Al-Sharatain, is described on pp. 39–42. For Sumerian planet names, Kasak and Veede 2001 is an accessible source; see also de Santillana and von Dechend 1969. The worldview shaped by classical astrology, with its pervasive sevenfold patterns, is well described in Lewis 1970.

CHAPTER TWO.
TWO NEW WORLDS

The story of the discovery of Uranus is recounted in Lemonick 2009, and that of Neptune in Standage 2000. For the status of astrology in the age of reason, Baker 2013, p. 339–411, gives a good overview. The claim that the discovery of Uranus struck a blow against astrology can be found, among other places, in McIntosh 1969, p. 86; ironically, Morrison's use of Uranus in mundane prediction can be found in the same book on p. 94. The quote from Alan Leo on p. 30 is from Leo 1983, p. 37. The scene from *Buddenbrooks* cited on page 34 is from Mann 1961, p. 150; the Neptunian nature of nineteenth-century political radicalism is well explored in Billington 1980. For "the way of the animal powers," see Campbell 1988.

CHAPTER THREE.
THE CEREAN ERA

The events leading to the discovery of Ceres are chronicled in Peebles 2000, pp. 5–9. The career of Ceres as a planet is discussed in Brown 2010, pp. 22–25. The best history of Romanticism remains Clark 1973.

Demetra George's book is currently available in an expanded edition; see George and Bloch 2003.

CHAPTER FOUR.
PHANTOMS OF HEAVEN

The story of Vulcan's discovery and disappearance has been ably covered in Baum and Sheehan 1997 and Levenson 2015. The strange history of the dark moon Lilith still awaits its chronicler; in the meantime, see Sepharial 1918 and Goldstein-Jacobson 1961. For Blavatsky's discussions of Vulcan, see Blavatsky 2010. For Bailey, Heindel, and Plummer, see Bailey 1951; Heindel 1909, pp. 420–25; and Khei X° 1920, pp. 20–21, 174, and 313. The descriptions of Lilith's influence cited in the text are from Sepharial 1918, pp. 38; Goldstein-Jacobson 1961, p. 6, and Foy 1988, p. 1. For the history of modern feminist witchcraft, Hutton 2000 is the standard account.

CHAPTER FIVE.
THE PLUTONIAN ERA

The history of Pluto's discovery and the pop-culture dimensions of Pluto's career are engagingly sketched out in Tyson 2009. The unknown presence near the fixed star Wasat is mentioned in George 1975, p. 324. The caution with which astrologers approached Pluto in the years immediately after its discovery is also found in George 1975, pp. 324–34; the quotation is from p. 324. Davis 1947 is an example of the uncritical cheerleading that proclaimed nuclear power as "energy too cheap to meter." Yenne 1986 is a good summary of the glory days of manned space travel; Clarke 1968 is a classic example of science fiction mistaking itself for science fact. For the transformation of Marxism into a Plutonian movement, Billington 2000 and Wilson 1940 are classic treatments. For the origins and early development of psychoanalysis, see Makari 2008. The H. P. Lovecraft quote is from his most famous tale, "The Call of Cthulhu;" see Lovecraft 1971, p. 1. The Bertrand Russell quote is from Russell 1918, pp. 47–48.

CHAPTER SIX.
THE TWILIGHT OF PLUTO

Charles Fort's comment about the construction of science's reputation is in Fort 1974, p. 318. The decline in estimates of Pluto's size may be found in Tyson 2009, pp. 25–28. The half-serious prediction of Pluto's impending demise is Dressler and Russell 1980; the disproof of the Planet X hypothesis is Standish 1993. The Time-Life books cited are respectively Bergamini 1962 and Frazier 1985.

Pope 2008 is a thorough summary of the WPPSS collapse and its impact on the nuclear power industry. Wohlforth and Hendrix 2016 is an example of the current round of cheerleading concerning space colonization. Compare its claims to Edwards 2005, Mann 2013, Mann 2014, Meyer 2020, and O'Bryan 2000, among many other publications on the radiation hazards of deep space. For the decline and fall of communism, Coleman 1996 and Pryce-Jones 1995 are useful.

Brown 1956 and Marcuse 1955 are typical of the pro-sexuality literature from mid-twentieth-century pundits. Among the most influential critiques of Freud and psychoanalysis are Crews 2017 and Masson 1984. The *New York Times Magazine* article cited on page 100 is Schwartz 2015; the INSERM study is INSERM Collective Expertise Center 2004.

For the role of sacred geometry in the early modern period, see Hancox 1992; for its modern revival, see especially Lawlor 1982 and Vandenbroeck 1987. Panero 2016 is a useful introduction to Jacob Collins and the revolt against modern art; for Alma Deutscher, her website at https://www.almadeutscher.com/ is the best starting place.

CHAPTER SEVEN.
AFTER PLUTO

The poems attributed to Ossian, interestingly enough, are beginning to see renewed interest now that Ceres is a dwarf planet and not merely an asteroid; see http://ossianonline.org/ for the National University of Ireland, Galway's efforts in this direction. The original article on the Kessler syndrome is Kessler and Cour-Palais 1978; while extensively discussed online, it remains largely absent from published books. For the implosion of the New Left in the United States, Mclellan and Avery 1977 remains a vivid narrative source. For phrenology, Van Wyhe 2011 is a very detailed and helpful source.

CHAPTER EIGHT.
THE COSMOS REBORN

The material on the Tree of Life discussed in this chapter may be compared helpfully with Fortune 1935. The discussion of the Initiation of the Nadir draws from this and also from Fortune 1966.

Bibliography

Ambler, Eric. 1936. *The Dark Frontier.* London: Hodder.

Aveni, Anthony F. 1989. *Empires of Time.* New York: Basic Books.

Bailey, Alice. 1951. *Esoteric Astrology.* New York: Lucis Trust.

Baker, Jim. 2013. *The Cunning Man's Handbook: The Practice of English Folk Magic 1550–1900.* London: Avalonia.

Baum, Richard, and Sheehan, William. 1997. *In Search of Planet Vulcan: The Ghost in Newton's Clockwork Machine.* New York: Plenum.

Bergamini, David. 1962. *The Universe.* New York: Time-Life Books.

Billington, James H. 1980. *Fire in the Minds of Men: Origins of the Revolutionary Faith.* New York: Basic Books.

Blavatsky, Helena P. 2010. *Secret Doctrine Commentaries.* Point Loma, Calif.: I.S.I.S. Foundation.

Brown, Mike. 2010. *How I Killed Pluto and Why It Had It Coming.* New York: Spiegel and Grau.

Brown, Norman O. 1959. *Life against Death.* Middletown, Conn.: Wesleyan University Press.

Burgoyne, Thomas. 1889. *The Light of Egypt.* San Francisco: Religio-Philosophical Publishing House.

Campbell, Joseph. 1988. *Historical Atlas of World Mythology, Volume 1: The Way of the Animal Powers.* New York: Harper & Row.

Chambers, Robert W. 1920. *The Slayer of Souls.* New York: George H. Dorran.

Clark, Kenneth. 1973. *The Romantic Rebellion.* New York: Harper & Row.

Clarke, Arthur C. 1968. *The Promise of Space.* New York: Harper & Row.

Coleman, Fred. 1996. *The Decline and Fall of the Soviet Empire.* New York: St. Martin's Press.

Cornell, James. 1981. *The First Stargazers*. New York: Scribner.

Crews, Frederick C. 2017. *Freud: The Making of an Illusion*. New York: Henry Holt.

Davis, Harry M. 1947. *Energy Unlimited: The Electron and Atom in Everyday Life*. New York: Murray Hill Books.

de Santillana, Giorgio, and Hertha von Dechend. 1969. *Hamlet's Mill*. Boston: Nonpareil Books.

Dijkstra, Bram. 1986. *Idols of Perversity*. Oxford: Oxford University Press.

Dressler, A. J., and C. T. Russell. 1980. "The Pending Disappearance of Pluto." *EOS* 61, no. 44, p. 690.

Edwards, Rob. August 2005. "Cosmic Rays May Prevent Long-Haul Space Travel." *New Scientist* 1.

Evans, James. 1998. *The History and Practice of Ancient Astronomy*. Oxford: Oxford University Press.

Fort, Charles. 1974. *The Complete Books of Charles Fort*. New York: Dover.

Fortune, Dion (Violet Firth Evans). 1966. *The Cosmic Doctrine*. Cheltenham, UK: Helios.

———. 1935. *The Mystical Qabalah*. London: Ernest Benn.

Foy, Catt. 1988. "Lilith—the Dark Moon." *The Second Road Newsletter*.

Frazier, Kendrick. *Solar System*. 1985. New York: Time-Life Books.

Gage, Matilda Joslyn. 1893. *Woman, Church and State*. New York: The Truth Seeker Company.

George, Demetra, and Douglas Bloch. 2003. *Asteroid Goddesses*. Lake Worth, Fla.: Nicolas-Hays.

George, Llewellyn. 1975. *A to Z Horoscope Maker and Delineator*. 11th edition. St. Paul, Minn.: Llewellyn Publications.

Ghyka, Matila. 2016. *The Golden Number*. Rochester, Vt.: Inner Traditions.

Goldstein-Jacobson, Ivy. 1961. *The Dark Moon Lilith*. Pasadena, Calif.: By the author.

Grossinger, Richard. 2014. *The Night Sky: Soul and Cosmos*. Berkeley, Calif.: North Atlantic Books.

Hambidge, Jay. 1926. *The Elements of Dynamic Symmetry*. New Haven, Conn.: Yale University Press.

Hancox, Joy. 1992. *The Byrom Collection*. London: Jonathan Cape.

Hawkins, Gerald S., and John B. White. 1965. *Stonehenge Decoded*. Garden City, N.Y.: Doubleday and Co.

Hawthorne, Nathaniel. 1978. *The Blithedale Romance*. New York: Norton.

Heggie, Douglas C. 1981. *Megalithic Science: Ancient Mathematics and Astrology in Northwest Europe*. London: Thames & Hudson.

Heindel, Max. 1909. *The Rosicrucian Cosmo-Conception*. Oceanside, Calif.: Rosicrucian Fellowship.

Heinlein, Robert A. 1961. *Stranger in a Strange Land*. New York: Putnam.

Hickey, Isabel M. 1973. *Pluto or Minerva: The Choice Is Yours*. Watertown, Mass.: Fellowship House Bookshop.

Horkheimer, Max, and Theodor Adorno. 1972. *Dialectic of Enlightenment*. Translated by John Cummings. New York: Herder & Herder.

Hutton, Ronald. 2000. *The Triumph of the Moon*. Oxford: Oxford University Press.

INSERM Collective Expertise Center. 2004. "Psychotherapy: Three Approaches Evaluated." *INSERM Collective Expert Reports*. Paris: Institut National de la Santé et de la Recherche Médicale.

Josephson-Storm, Jason. 2017. *The Myth of Disenchantment: Magic, Modernity, and the Birth of the Human Sciences*. Chicago: University of Chicago Press.

Jung, Carl G. 1960. *Synchronicity: An Acausal Connecting Principle*. Translated by R. F. C. Hull. Princeton, N.J.: Princeton University Press.

Kasak, Enn, and Raul Veede, "Understanding Planets in Ancient Mesopotamia," Folklore 16, n.p., http://haldjas.folklore.ee/folklore; downloaded 30 September 2021.

Kessler, Donald J., and Burton G. Cour-Palais. 1978. "Collision Frequency of Artificial Satellites: The Creation of a Debris Belt." *Journal of Geophysical Research* 83: 2637–46.

Khei X° (George Winslow Plummer). 1920. *Rosicrucian Fundamentals*. New York: Flame Press.

Krupp, Edwin C. 1983. *Echoes of the Ancient Skies: The Astronomy of Lost Civilizations*. New York: Harper & Row.

Kuhn, Thomas S. 1970. *The Structure of Scientific Revolutions*. Chicago: University of Chicago Press.

Lawlor, Robert. 1982. *Sacred Geometry: Philosophy and Practice*. New York: Thames & Hudson.

Lemonick, Michael D. 2009. *The Georgian Star*. New York: W.W. Norton & Co.

Leo, Alan. 1983. *How to Judge a Nativity*. New York: Astrologer's Library.

Levenson, Thomas. 2015. *The Hunt for Vulcan*. New York: Random House.

Lewis, C. S. 1938. *Out of the Silent Planet*. London: The Bodley Head.

——. 1970. *The Discarded Image.* Cambridge: Cambridge University Press.

Lovecraft, H. P. 1971. *Tales of the Cthulhu Mythos.* Vol. 1. New York: Ballantine.

Makari, George. 2008. *Revolution in Mind: The Creation of Psychoanalysis.* New York: HarperCollins.

Mann, Adam. 2013. "Radiation Risk for Mars Astronauts Will Be Dangerously High." *Wired,* May 30, 2013.

——. 2014. "Space Radiation Remains Major Hazard for Humans Going to Mars." *Wired.*

Mann, Thomas. 1961. *Buddenbrooks.* New York: Vintage.

Marcuse, Herbert. 1955. *Eros and Civilization.* Boston: Beacon Press.

Masson, Jeffrey Moussaieff. 1984. *The Assault on Truth: Freud's Suppression of the Seduction Theory.* New York: Farrar, Straus and Giroux.

McIntosh, Christopher. 1969. *The Astrologers and their Creed: An Historical Outline.* New York: Praeger.

Mclellan, Vin, and Paul Avery. 1977. *The Voices of Guns.* New York: Putnam.

Meyer, Nicholas, ed. *The Health Risks of Extraterrestrial Environments.* https://three.jsc.nasa.gov/, accessed October 14, 2020.

North, John David. 2008. *Cosmos: An Illustrated History of Astronomy and Cosmology.* Chicago: University of Chicago Press.

O'Bryan, Martha, ed. 2000. "The Natural Space Radiation Hazard." *Radiation Effects and Analysis,* https://radhome.gsfc.nasa.gov/radhome/Nat_Space_Rad_Haz.htm, accessed October 14, 2020.

Panero, James. Winter 2016. "The New Old Masters." *City Journal,* https://www.city-journal.org/html/new-old-masters-14188.html, accessed October 14, 2020.

Peebles, Curtis. 2000. *Asteroids: A History.* Washington, D.C.: Smithsonian Institution Press.

Pope, Daniel. 2008. *Nuclear Implosions: The Rise and Fall of the Washington Public Power Supply System.* Cambridge: Cambridge University Press.

Pryce-Jones, David. 1995. *The Strange Death of the Soviet Empire.* New York: Henry Holt.

Rose, Michael. 2001. *Ugly as Sin.* Manchester, N.H.: Sophia Institute Press.

Roth, Philip. 1969. *Portnoy's Complaint.* New York: Random House.

Russell, Bertrand. 1918. *Mysticism and Logic and Other Essays.* London: Longmans Green.

Schwartz, Casey. June 28, 2015. "Tell It About Your Mother." *The New York Times Magazine.*

Sepharial (Walter Gorn Old). 1918. *The Science of Foreknowledge*. London: Foulsham.

Sheldrake, Rupert. 1981. *A New Science of Life*. London: Blond & Briggs.

Sibley, Ebenezer. 1826. *A New and Complete Illustration of the Celestial Science of Astrology*. London: By the Proprietor, at No. 17 Ave Maria Lane, St. Paul's.

Souden, David. 1997. *Stonehenge Revealed*. New York: Facts on File.

Standage, Tom. 2000. *The Neptune File*. New York: Walker & Co.

Standish, E. Myles, Jr. 1993. "Planet X: No Dynamical Evidence in the Optical Observations." *Astronomical Journal*.

St.-Germain, Comte de (Edgar de Valcourt-Vermont). 1901. *Practical Astrology*. Chicago: Laird & Lee.

Tarnas, Richard. 2006. *Cosmos and Psyche: Intimations of a New World View*. New York: Viking.

Tudge, Colin. 1999. *Neanderthals, Bandits and Farmers: How Agriculture Really Began*. New Haven, Conn.: Yale University Press.

Tyson, Neil deGrasse. 2009. *The Pluto Files: The Rise and Fall of America's Favorite Planet*. New York: W.W. Norton.

Vandenbrouck, André. 1987. *Philosophical Geometry*. Rochester, Vt.: Inner Traditions.

Van Wyhe, John. 2011. "The History of Phrenology on the Web."

Warnock, Christopher. 2006. *The Mansions of the Moon*. Iowa City, Ia.: Renaissance Astrology.

Weber, Max. 2009. *The Protestant Ethic and the Spirit of Capitalism*. Translated by Talcott Parsons. New York: Norton.

Wender, Dorothea, trans. 1973. "Works and Days." In *Hesiod and Theognis*. New York: Penguin.

Wilson, Edmund. 1940. *To the Finland Station*. New York: Harcourt, Brace.

Wohlforth, Charles P., and Amanda R. Hendrix. 2016. *Beyond Earth: Our Path to a New Home in the Planets*. New York: Pantheon Books.

Yenne, Bill. 1986. *The Astronauts: The First 25 Years of Manned Space Flight*. New York: Exeter Books.

Index

BOOKS OF RELATED INTEREST

The King in Orange
The Magical and Occult Roots of Political Power
by John Michael Greer

Alchemical Tantric Astrology
The Hidden Order of Seven Metals, Seven Planets, and Seven Chakras
by Frederick Hamilton Baker

Astrology for Mystics
Exploring the Occult Depths of the Water Houses in Your Natal Chart
by Tayannah Lee McQuillar

360 Degrees of Your Star Destiny
A Zodiac Oracle
by Ellias Lonsdale

Egregores
The Occult Entities That Watch Over Human Destiny
by Mark Stavish

Occulture
The Unseen Forces That Drive Culture Forward
by Carl Abrahamsson
Foreword by Gary Lachman

John Dee and the Empire of Angels
Enochian Magick and the Occult Roots of the Modern World
by Jason Louv

Astrology in Ancient Mesopotamia
The Science of Omens and the Knowledge of the Heavens
by Michael Baigent

INNER TRADITIONS • BEAR & COMPANY
P.O. Box 388 • Rochester, VT 05767
1-800-246-8648 • www.InnerTraditions.com

Or contact your local bookseller